Caribbean Chronicles

Dead Calm, Bone Dry

Eddie Jones

DEAD CALM, BONE DRY BY EDDIE JONES

Published by Illuminate YA an Imprint of Lighthouse Publishing of the Carolinas
2333 Barton Oaks Dr., Raleigh, NC, 27614

ISBN 978-1-946016-08-9
Copyright © 2017 by Eddie Jones
Cover design by Elaina Lee, www.forthemusedesign.com
Interior design by Atritex, www.atritex.com

Available in print from your local bookstore, online, or from the publisher at: www.LPCbooks.com

For more information on this book and the author visit: caribbeanchronicles.com & eddiejones.org

All rights reserved. Non-commercial interests may reproduce portions of this book without the express written permission of Lighthouse Publishing of the Carolinas, provided the text does not exceed 500 words. When reproducing text from this book, include the following credit line: "*Dead Calm, Bone Dry* by Eddie Jones published by Lighthouse Publishing of the Carolinas. Used by permission."

Commercial interests: No part of this publication may be reproduced in any form, stored in a retrieval system, or transmitted in any form by any means—electronic, photocopy, recording, or otherwise—without prior written permission of the publisher, except as provided by the United States of America copyright law.

This is a work of fiction. Names, characters, and incidents are all products of the author's imagination or are used for fictional purposes. Any mentioned brand names, places, and trademarks remain the property of their respective owners, bear no association with the author or the publisher, and are used for fictional purposes only.

Brought to you by the creative team at Lighthouse Publishing of the Carolinas: Rowena Kuo, Shonda Savage, Christy Distler, and Brian Cross.

Library of Congress Cataloging-in-Publication Data
Jones, Eddie.
Dead Calm, Bone Dry / Eddie Jones 1st ed.

Printed in the United States of America

What Others Are Saying About The Caribbean Chronicles Series

"Gave this five stars. Recommend for all ages. Great descriptive fantasy. Loved it."

~ Amazon review

"Hope to see the search continue. Characters are growing and gaining strength. Let the search begin and see what new adventure barbecue and barnacle can get into."

~ Amazon review

"Action packed, fast paced, full of intrigue and suspense! What more could you ask for in a book. The Caribbean Chronicles series is written as a YA, but as an adult I loved it. You'll dive deep into the life of a pirate at sea, the crew at the mercy of the Captain's will. Full of adventure and humor, this is a great read."

~ Amazon review

DEDICATION

Dead Calm, Bone Dry is dedicated to Spencer Wyatt and all those impacted by epilepsy. Learn how you can make a difference by visiting: www.epilepsy.com/make-difference

Contents

Ship's Log On a Tight Dead Line 1
1. Some Fellows On Trial For Piracy 9
2. A Surprising Witness 17
3. Caught in the In Between 25
4. Out-of-Body Experience 39
5. Going to See a Dog about a Treasure 47
6. The Man with the Eye Patch 53
7. We hatch a plan to steal a treasure 57
8. The Dead Calm, Bone Dry 65
9. I steal a ship 69
10. Dog Gone It! 71
11. The Scary-looking woman 77
12. Dead in the Water 83
13. The Phantom Ship 89
14. castaways 93
15. Soul Survivors 97
16. First Day as castaways 101
17. Day Two Adrift at Sea 103

18.	The Flying Dutchman	105
19.	Lost	111
20.	Coffin Cay	115
21.	Funeral for a Friend	117
22.	A Surprise atop The Skull	121
23.	Caved In	129
24.	At the End of My Rope	135
25.	Dead Men Tell Tales	139
26.	The Secret Place	145
27.	Back from the Dead	149
28.	Fake Flakes Fall on Graceland	151
	Ship's Log Isla de Ataúd	155

Ship's Log
On a Tight Dead Line

The leaky, wooden ship bashed into another wave, sending a shudder down the length of its hull. I clung tightly to the bars of my prison cell and studied the places where iron shackles had worn my skin raw. Another rush of salty bilge water sloshed up my calves and receded, stinging my open wounds. The ship's brig reeked of urine and feces.

In the cell across from me, William Shakespeare rested in a threadbare hammock strung beneath two sagging support beams. A single candle wedged into a knotty hole illuminated his portly face and owlish eyes. With a quill in one hand and writing journal in the other, my "scribe" looked exactly as I remembered his picture on the front cover of *Romeo and Juliet*.

"How long will it take?"

William Shakespeare paused from his scribe scribbling to peer at me through the bars. "Dost thou inquire as to how long it takes to expire? Verily I say, when it comes to swinging by the neck, 'tis hard to know. Hath seen some jerk and twitch for a minute or more. Gruesome business, hanging, and a horrid way to meet one's maker."

"I meant how long before this ship reaches Port Charles?"

"Oh, that." He laid aside the journal and gazed upwards at the ceiling. "From the rattling of those sails, not long. Sounds as if our captain hath sighted land."

"You can stop with the 'thees' and 'thous' and 'thines.' This isn't the Globe Theatre in London, and you're not the real William Shakespeare."

"Why sayest thou that?"

"Because you're not, okay? I bet the real Shakespeare never set foot on a pirate ship."

"Detractors and scoffers and critics ... the world 'tis a cruel crowd, indeed." He pointed the quill at my feet. "Want that I should draw a picture of them vermin nibbling at your toesies? Would only take a moment to add the illustration."

I studied the rats torpedoing through the swill of dank water. They were not too bad, but every once in a while, one of them bit my leg. "Mom hates rats. And snakes. Spiders freak her out, too."

"Aye, mums can be like that, they can."

"Read me my note to Mom."

Clearing his throat, William Shakespeare began.

Dear Mom: I'm still sailing around the Caribbean exploring beautiful beaches, haunted forts, dangerous dungeons, and mysterious lakes fed by underground rivers. Sorry I fell into that creek and drowned. You told me to be careful, and I tried, but I guess I wasn't careful enough.

"Are thou quite certain thou drowned? Could it not be thou experienced that other thing thou mentioned?"

"An absence seizure? Maybe. I mean, I did and that's what caused me to fall into the creek, but then I came out of it. At least I thought I did. And besides, petit mals only last a few seconds. Never had one last this long."

"But how can you be sure you're not having one right now? Thou said one cannot tell when thou is in a trance."

"Can you just read the letter, please?"

Remember last spring how the two of us worried about my pre-SAT scores? You kept saying they weren't good enough, and I'd never get into college unless I did better. We spent hours working on those writing prompts and practicing, remember that?

'What is something you dislike about yourself?'

'What is something you do well?'

'What is your favorite television show and why?'

No need to worry now, Mom. The ship I'm sailing on leaves me with plenty of time to practice writing essays.

"You know ... 'tis me wielding the quill."

"My story. My obituary."

"Aye, 'tis that."

"Besides, I'd write the letter myself if I could."

William Shakespeare's furrowed brow melted as he gave me a sympathetic look. "Must be painful having thy wrists bound in such a fashion. No doubt thou will think twice before taking another swing at Horrible Horace."

"Who?"

"The jailor who brought thee aboard."

"He shouldn't have clubbed me."

"Simply taking adequate precautions, he was. Cuffing a pirate is dangerous business. 'Specially one with all his limbs and teeth."

"I'm not a pirate. Pirates are lying, murdering thieves who get drunk, chase women, and say things like, 'Aaaarrrrgggghhhh,' 'avast, me hearty matey,' and 'swab the deck, ye scurvy dog.'"

"Those be harsh words for a dandy lad who is fast on his way to wearing a noose necktie. I dare say thy mum would be heartbroken to learn thou hast taken to consorting with knaves and scallywags."

"You know, for someone whose only job is to write down what I say, you do a lot of interrupting."

Sighing loudly, my scribe continued.

I think I mentioned in my last letter how I had taken possession of a ship, the Black Avenger. That's her name—Black Avenger. My scribe says a ship is called "her" because it has a wide, round bottom and demands constant attention.

"I am not a scribe," my scribe said. "I am an amanuensis."

"A what?"

"Secretary."

"A fancily dressed pirate is what you are. Read on."

DEAD CALM, BONE DRY

My ship is on the hard right now. That's what we call a vessel that's not in the water. I accidentally ran aground on a sandbar near Don't Rock Reef. Don't Rock Reef is at the entrance to Looney Dunes Lagoon and not far from Peter Pan's Port. I know these places sound like some cheesy theme park attractions, but they're real places. I'm including a map with this letter, so you can see all the places I've been. I would have sent postcards from each port, but postcards haven't been invented yet. Might look into that as a business opportunity later.

I accidently ran the Black Avenger *aground and needed time to fix the hole in the hull. But my crew was getting restless, so I came up with the idea of building a golf course. Figured that would keep them distracted while I fixed my ship. Didn't work out like I'd hoped.*

Remember that picture Grandpa took of his TV when the Apollo 11 landed on the moon? You had it in that photo album with my baby picture—the one that burned up in our apartment fire? You know how on the back of the picture, Grandpa had written: "The Eagle has landed." Well, not on my golf course, it hasn't. Not a single member of my crew could make eagle, birdie, or par.

"Is thy mum going to know what thou means by golf? Shouldest thou not call it links?"

"Golf is a thing where I'm from. Keep going."

I named the golf course the Sea of Tranquility because the first tee sits at the base of a volcano that looks a lot like that picture Grandpa took. To have any chance at all of reaching the green in two, you have to clear a really wide lava flow that cuts across the fairway. We lose a lot of golf balls on that hole. Or did. Now that I'm not there to take care of the course, no telling who's in charge of golf balls. I was the only one who knew how to soak the turtle eggs in the sulfur pond. Leave them in too long and they get hard as rocks and snap the head right off a driver.

You would think after I went to the trouble of laying out a golf course and adding those huts around the lagoon and constructing a boardwalk to the waterfall that my crew would be grateful, but instead, they fired me.

Or, I should say, fired "on" me. I managed to escape by swimming out past the surf zone. My plan was to sneak back to the Black Avenger after it got dark, but I got picked up by the crew of a Dutch frigate, and now I'm on my way to Port Charles.

My scribe uncorked his flask and took a long sip of rum. He uncorked his flask a lot. "Dost thou wish for me to mention how thou saw the *Flying Dutchman*?"

"There's no such ship."

"Oh? What vessel 'tis it that be sailed by the dead, demons, and souls of the cursed?"

"A pirate like yourself would hope there's a ship like that."

"I am a poet and playwright, not a pirate."

"Ah, yes, the famous William Shakespeare of Stratford-upon-Avon. Like anyone is going to believe that."

"Dost thou wish that I recite a few lines? 'To be, or not to be—'"

"And you be out of time!" Our jailor said, sloshing his way down the narrow passageway that separated the two rows of cells. "Deckhand called down ter say we's puttin' into port. That means you two swabs best be gettin' yer affairs in order. Ah'll be back fer you two in a jiffy."

William Shakespeare waited until the jailor is out of earshot before whispering to me, "I've sailed aboard her."

"Aboard who?"

"Not who, what. *The Flying Dutchman*."

"You've sailed aboard a ship crewed by the dead?" He nodded. "Well, it seems to me a ship sailed by ghosts could have kept a dead playwright from getting captured by a prison ship."

"Doth not work like that. There are rules for the deceased, same as for the living, and one of them is never make fun of demonic rulers. You see, I penned this play about a despot. That is a dictator with a—"

"I know what despot is. The word was on my Honors English exam."

"Right. Very well, then. A few of the gents aboard the *Dutchman* were rehearsing their lines. Ivan the Terrible, Attila the Hun, Genghis Khan ... Jack Black."

"Hang on. You sailed with the actor Jack Black?"

"I only knew him as the tanner from Bristol. Lovely chap with a dark sense of humor. Skins folks and makes designer handbags from their hide. Popular with all the ladies. Sells them in the shops of London under names like Gilbert Gucci, Lewis Vuitton, and Prada."

"Those are his brands?"

My scribe shook his head. "Names of the folks he's skinned. Now old Jack, he happened to mention that he thought the queen was so large he could make three handbags out of her hide. Should not hath said that. First rule of humor is never let a good joke go to thy head, and he did. Lost his, too. His head, I mean. Nasty business the guillotine. Later while I was expounding upon Hamlet's character arc and the principles of the basic three-act plot structure, the captain of the Dutchman happened by. Nasty oaf named Pompous Pilate. Hates Jews and Greeks and, apparently, British playwrights. Next thing I knew, he'd tossed me in the water, and the *Dutchman* was sailing away. I managed to fetch ashore on a small island just off Tortuga. With such a girth, I float exceedingly well."

He said this while patting his ample belly.

"A few days later, Horrible Horace comes into the grog shop where I am performing a one-man soliloquy and sees the word 'pyrate' stamped on my wrist. Tosses me into this brig, which is how I came to be aboard this ship."

"Interesting story. And long with maybe too many details. Maybe you should think about becoming a writer."

"Am! I am a writer!"

A few cells down from us, I heard Horrible Horace rattling his keys, unlocking doors, and gathering prisoners. "Can we get on with my letter? We're about to run out of time."

I'm not writing to tell you about my golf game, Mom, or how much fun I'm having, even though I was hitting my driver pretty good before my crew chased me off the island. Dad would be proud to know I've taken up golf. I think you told me one time how much he enjoyed playing.

In fact, Dad is the reason I'm writing this letter. Some months back, I met an old fisherman who says he sailed with Dad. Crazy, right? I mean Dad hasn't even been born yet. But then I'm here, sailing around with pirates, and I haven't been born yet, either.

Anyway, if you want to say a prayer for me, that'd be great. I know sometimes, praying makes you feel better. Plus, I have a hunch where I'm going I'll need all the help I can get.

Love, Ricky.

Right then cell door opened. Horrible Horace stepped inside and grabbed me roughly by the hair, yanking me into the hallway.

"The instructions," I called back to my scribe. "What about those?"

To the person or persons who find this message in a bottle, you will see where I drew the perforation lines above this section. Fold the page along the dots. It should tear cleanly.

Please give this letter to my mother. She lives on the western shore of the Chesapeake Bay in a town called Quiet Cove. I don't know her new address. Our apartment burned down last week. Or maybe it burned down last month. It's hard to know how long I've been sailing around in the Caribbean Sea.

Mom drives an eighteen-wheeler. Can't be too many of those parked around Quiet Cove. Last name Bradshaw. When you find Mom, tell her not to worry. Tell her I'm sailing around the Caribbean islands, surfing reef breaks, and writing a best-selling novel about pirates.

Thanks, Ricky Bradshaw

My *amanuensis* ripped pages from his writing ledger, rolled them tightly, and slipped them into an empty rum bottle: corked it, and shoved the bottle through a hole in the hull.

"Littering's a ten-guinea fine."

"Add it to my tab," said William Shakespeare. Rolling out of his hammock, he stood and straightened his shirtsleeves, threaded cuff links, and tucked his shirt's tail into the waistband of black britches. I have to admit, with his receding hairline and bushy gray beard, he did look a little like the famous British author.

He stuck out his arms and said to the jailor, "Brutus, my bracelets, please?"

Horrible Horace grunted and tied my scribe's wrists, then pulled William Shakespeare into the hallway next to me.

"Don't you two try any funny business," Horrible Horace warned. "This pistol's loaded with solid shot. I'd hate to deny the two of you a fair hearing."

"Fair hearing indeed," scoffed my scribe. "A noose necktie will be our reward for standing before the commodore."

"If we're innocent, we have nothing to worry about." Sometimes I say stupid stuff like that.

"Verily I say, many a dandy lad has had similar thoughts and found himself dancing with the Devil at the end of a short rope."

"Look alive, you two," Horrible Horace barked. "Leastways while you still can."

And with that I marched off to be tried for piracy.

CHAPTER ONE

SOME FELLOWS ON TRIAL FOR PIRACY

From the deck of the Dutch frigate, I looked onto the wide blue bay filled with ships and boats of all sizes. Below us, dockhands scurried along the wharf, unloading cargo onto wooden carts. Farther down the street, stately men in white straw hats exited carriages. Not far from the edge of a seawall, tents made from sails were strung between palm trees, providing shade for the men lounging about on the beach. I might have appreciated the view more if ropes had not bound my wrists and ankles.

Horrible Horace ordered us to wait along the ship's railing while he directed a clot of shabbily dressed boys and girls down the gangplank. Like us, they were bound hand and foot.

"Don't tell me those kids were picked up for piracy," I said. "Most don't even look old enough to be in school."

"Orphans and runaways, most likely. Black Spot runs a tight ship. No room for riffraff and ruffians on his watch."

"Who's Black Spot?"

"Commodore Blackburn Chamberlin Spotswood, nephew of the governor's wife. Any who is a lost boy or girl and doth appear healthy is shipped off to work in the sugarcane fields. The diseased and deformed face a more gruesome fate."

I blinked away sweat and swiped my forehead while imagining what it must be like to work in sugarcane fields in the tropics. "What could be worse than working all day in this heat?"

"I dare say thou may find out soon enough."

After the boys and girls were herded into a circular livestock pen and left under guard by British soldiers, Horrible Horace clomped back up the gangplank.

"Welcome back, my lord," said William Shakespeare.

"Stop calling me that!"

"As you wish, Your Royal Hyenas."

"You first," said Horrible Horace, jabbing me in the back with his pistol. "And don't you try to run."

"Wouldn't dare think of it," I said.

Running was absolutely what I was thinking.

"Williams in the bay love it when prisoners run. Feed 'em breakfast, I do."

I'll skip over the boring, sight-seeing stuff that happened next. Basically we walked down cobblestone streets, passing taverns and drunks and boarding houses: and a livery stable with horses, and quite possibly drunk horses. (Some young boys were emptying jugs into troughs, and the horses were lapping it up and stumbling around.) Eventually we ended up in front of a narrow wooden door at the base of a cliff. On top of the cliff was a fort.

Horrible Horace pounded his fat fist on the door. The door opened partway. A yellow eye looked out.

Horrible Horace grabbed me by the hair and jerked me forward. "Pirate!"

The yellow eye swiveled, studied me, and the door opened all the way. The man with the yellow eye shoved a lit torch into my hand and disappeared.

I'll skip all the boring stuff about how we climbed up a stone staircase and emerged into a large underground cavern illuminated by torches mounted on damp walls. I won't even hardly mention the torture equipment positioned around the humongous cavern chamber. Except to say it looked a lot like a fitness workout gym, only instead of weights and stuff there was The Rack, Breaking Wheel, and Knee Splitter.

William Shakespeare caught me gawking at a leather cage. "Victim is placed inside with only his head protruding from the webbing. The cage is doth hoisted over the brow of a cliff. All manner of birds have a go at the prisoner's head until all that remains of the poor soul is a bloody skull. Beastly way to go."

"Stop yer jawing and get ter walking."

I'll skip more boring stuff like how we passed through the "chamber of horrors" as my scribe described them and wove our way around a section of walled catacombs filled with prison cells where desperate men, filthy and stinking, flung themselves at prison bars, screaming to be set free.

"See, lad? There art worse things than swinging by thy neck. These are the ones who doth begged for mercy and received that and more."

Finally we reached a part of the fort that actually looked like something you expect to see in a fort. By this I mean, it had walls that were not made from rocks and a door positioned in a wooden doorframe that was not mounted into stone.

With a hard shove in the back, Horrible Horace shoved me onto the fort's parade grounds. Soldiers stood in formation with muskets at their sides. In the center of the compound, a Union Jack fluttered atop a flagpole. Two wooden lecterns flanked the flagpole. Behind one stood a well-dressed man in a red tailcoat, black breeches, and white stockings. White curls sprouted from beneath his black tricorn hat. Behind the other lectern were two scruffy-looking men: both shabbily dressed.

I recognize the two shabbily dressed men: they had been aboard the *Black Avenger* the day I'd been captured. Then, their loud bragging of robbing ships and killing crew had sounded brash. Now, both look terrified. It was easy to see why. A set of gallows stood in one corner of the fort. Atop the scaffolding, a burly man wearing a leather mask stood with arms folded. Behind him, a pair of nooses swung gently with the breeze.

An officer, much younger than those seated on the long bench, rose from his chair.

"Black Spot," William Shakespeare whispered to me.

Commodore Spotswood was dressed in a dark blue jacket with gold mortarboards on the shoulders. Brooding eyes peered out from beneath the brim of a tricorn hat. "Has the jury reached a verdict?"

"We have, sir."

"And how do you judge?"

"We, the jury, find the defendants, Charles Pugh and Brody Greaves … guilty of piracy."

A groan escaped from a shaggy-haired defendant. The taller one remained rigid, his stone-hard eyes unwavering as he fixed his stare on the gallows.

"Do either of you wish to make a statement before judgment is passed?"

The flag fluttered; birds squawked. From far away, came the sound of booming surf.

"Very well. Charles Pugh and Brody Greaves, inasmuch as you have been found guilty of piracy, the punishment for which is death, it is hereby the opinion of this court that you should—"

"I got something ter say," said the defendant Greaves.

"Oh, this ought to be rich," William Shakespeare said to me.

"I wan' ter say that I ne'er got a fair trial. These proceedings is a shame and a travesty. In all me days of sailin', I ain' ne're set foot aboard a pirate ship. I served the queen faithfully all me days, I 'ave. I'm just a poor seaman who's lost his way, is all."

The commodore's face remains unchanged. "Anything else?"

"'Tis true I was aboard the *Black Avenger*, I don' deny it. But was there against me will, I was."

"And the other pirates you sailed with," the commodore said. "Did they hold you against your will in the grog shop on Santa Maria, too?"

Snickers erupted from some of the soldiers. The commodore looked at the defendant the way my mom looks at cockroaches right before she steps on them.

"Aye! Was their prisoner, I was! Tried to leave, but they would have none of it."

"And I suppose you would have us believe these men forced you to drink rum, steal gold, silver and jewels, and go cavorting about the streets of Petit-Goâve with wenches and tramps?"

The soldiers' snickering turned into out-loud laughter.

"He was there! He seen how it was." He pointed at me.

This was not the sort of pirate trial help I was looking for at that moment.

"Is this true?" the commodore asked, now looking at me the way my mom looks at bird poop on her car. "Do you know this man, Brody Greaves?"

"Tell 'em! Tell 'em how it was, mate. You was there."

"Man axed ye a question," Horrible Horace said, pushing me forward.

At that moment I did not exactly like my chances of staying alive.

"For gawd's sake, boy, speak up fer yer old shipmates. Tell 'em how we didn' 'ave no choice in the matter. It's yer neck that's on the line, too!"

"I, ah ... wasn't in the grog shop on Santa Maria with you that night," I said. "I mean, I was in the grog shop, but only for a few minutes. And the only time I saw you was on the ship."

"Liar! Coward! You were there! Thick as thieves we was. Rot in hell, ye will fer lying. Swear it!"

"Pay him no mind!" William Shakespeare called, trying to comfort me. "His curses cannot reach thee from the grave."

But I wasn't so sure. The doctor aboard the *Black Avenger* had warned that if I stayed with the ship I would die a pirate's death. And now I was being charged with piracy.

"You?" the commodore asked "Any final words?"

Charles Pugh refused to look up. His stringy brown hair hid his face. I couldn't be sure but I think he was crying.

"Very well. Inasmuch as each of you has been found guilty of piracy, the penalty for which is death, it is hereby the judgment of this tribunal that you be hanged by the neck until dead. May God have mercy on your souls."

The sound of the gavel echoed across the courtyard.

The drummer began beating out a melancholy cadence.

Soldiers grabbed both defendants and hauled them across the grassy parade grounds toward the gallows.

"Traitor! Liar! Same as yer dad, you are," Greaves yelled at me. "And you'll go the way of that scoundrel, Richard Bradshaw, too!"

"That one has a tongue on him," William Shakespeare said.

"Did you hear what he said? He knows my dad. How can he know Dad?"

"I wouldst not put much stock in the ranting of a thief pounding on death's door. Cheat the hangman and live to fight another day. That be the course thou shouldst sail, now."

Before I could ask what he meant by cheat the hangman, Greaves called out, "A prayer! For gawd's sake, somebody pray for ma soul!"

But no prayer was offered. Only the squawking of gulls circling the gallows interrupted the two pirates' shuffling of bare feet on the gallows. The hangman positioned a noose over Greaves' head, then slid it down, removing all slack so that his heels barely touch the planking. Doing the same with Pugh, he then grasped a humongous lever and waited for a signal from the commodore.

Pugh's sobs were drowned out by the drummers' drum roll.

The commodore nodded; the hangman shoved the lever forward.

The men fell.

There was a sharp crack, like the sound of a bullwhip striking wet pavement. Pugh's legs jerked; his feet twitched. After several minutes, his spasmodic convulsions cease.

Greaves suffered longer, thrashing violently. Eventually he, too, stopped jerking.

The pair twisted slowly with the sea breeze. Scaffolding boards creaked. Above them came the mocking cries of gulls circling the gallows.

"NEXT!"

Horrible Horace shoved me with the end of his Turtle Billy club; I took my place behind the lectern.

CHAPTER TWO

A Surprising Witness

I expected William Shakespeare to join me at the lectern. I mean, he was the one with the word "pyrate" tattooed into his arm, not me. But as I looked onto the sea of red uniforms, I saw my scribe slinking away.

"You there," called the commodore. "Come forward and take your place with the other defendant."

"If it pleases Your Excellency, I'll be waiting for me legal counsel."

"Legal counsel? What bar-fly barrister would agree to represent the likes of you?"

"Potter is his name. Jolly chap. Hails from Gloucester, I believe."

"Percy Potter? Why, he's little more than a pirate himself."

"Privateer," William Shakespeare countered, "and a first rate gunner. Leastways, that's what I hear."

The commodore leaned forward and placed his fists on the desk. "Well, if he shows his face in Port Charles, he'll be arrested and tried for his crimes, of that you can be sure."

"Still, if it's all the same, Most High and Exalted Eminence, I would prefer that thou dispatch with the lad first. And if thou can spare a spot of rum for me parched throat, I would be much obliged."

"Your throat will be massaged soon enough with rope." Shifting his focus, the commodore nodded to the crown prosecutor.

"Ricky Bradshaw, you are charged with kidnapping, piracy, bribery, accessory to bribery, extortion, assault, battery …"

"He means the shooting of cannons," William Shakespeare said.

"You, sir, keep quiet!" said the commodore.

"Disorderly conduct, disturbing the peace, conspiracy to commit murder, forgery, fraud, aiding and abetting …"

"Technically, Your Nefarious Nobility, gambling is not an offense in these parts."

The commodore waggled a finger at William Shakespeare. "One more word, and I'll have you drawn and quartered. Do I make myself clear?"

William Shakespeare made a zipping motion across his mouth.

"Vandalism, perjury, harassment, haggling, and stealing goats." He looked up from his reading. "How does the defendant plead?"

Thank goodness I have the lectern to lean on. If not, I might have collapsed under the weight of the charges.

"Not guilty."

"Speak louder."

"I'M INNOCENT!"

"We'll see about that," said the commodore, making a note in his ledger.

"In addition to the testimony you heard moments ago from a convicted pirate who placed the defendant in a grog shop on Santa Maria and in the company of a crew of pirates," the crown prosecutor said, "we have numerous soldiers who will swear that they saw the defendant in the company of Thaddeus LaFoote, a known pirate and enemy of the crown. Further, these witnesses will attest to the fact that the defendant abducted the governor's daughter."

"I didn't abduct her. She came with me willingly."

"We shall see about that. Sir, as my first witness I call Rebecca Evaline Vance to the stand."

WHOA! Rebecca? Seriously?

I confess: I could feel my heart pounding pretty hard. Rebecca was only, like, the prettiest girl I'd met in pirate land. Actually, she was pretty much the only girl I'd met in pirate land. And I hadn't seen her since I wrecked the *Black Avenger* and swam away to avoid the crew. The fact that she might be at my trial, well … that was good news. She could vouch for me.

Rebecca came striding towards me wearing a white hoop dress. Sun-bleached curls bounced beneath a white lace bonnet; her cheeks were butternut brown from her Caribbean islands tan. Never had I seen anyone so beautiful.

Marching up to me she pointed at a nasty scar that ran from her wrist to thumb. "How dare you leave me marooned on that dreadful island with those savages."

SLAP!

"Do you have any idea what I went through after you left?"

SLAP! SLAP!

"I had to barricade myself in a cave to keep the crew from having their way with me. And you call yourself chivalrous and brave."

"I, ah … meant to come back for you. Honest, I did."

"And yet you did not. By the way, those golf balls?"

"They hatched. Baby tortoises crawling all over the place."

I couldn't help but smile as I pictured tiny turtles sunning on the fairways.

"Thank goodness the commodore spotted me with his spyglass; otherwise, I might still be on that island with those beastly men."

I tried to think of something I could say, some way to let her know how sorry I was, but all I could muster is a weak, "Sorry."

She snatched the medallion I had given her from her neck and threw it at me. "Why I ever thought you could be trusted, I will never know."

She pivoted and marched off, leaving me feeling sick to my stomach. So her testimony wasn't exactly the good news I'd hoped for.

"Finally, we have the written statement of the merchant captain who captured the defendant." The crown prosecutor was back to presenting his case against me. "He will state that he saw the *Black Avenger* moored in a cove near where the accused was picked up."

"Beached," I explained. "The Avenger was more like hard aground than anchored."

"So you admit you were in possession of a pirate's ship?"

"I ... ah ... yes."

"Would you like to change your plea to guilty?" asked the commodore.

"Would it matter?"

"Do not take that tone with me, boy."

"Boy?" I wanted to say. "Why, you're not much older than I am." You probably already figured this out: I didn't like the commodore.

"What difference does it make if I confess to something I didn't do?"

"A guilty plea will not spare you the noose, nor should it. But if you confess now and save us time, I shall order the rope be lengthened. This ensures that your neck snaps and you die quickly."

"I still say I'm not a pirate."

The crown prosecutor said, "Do you admit to being aboard a pirate ship and taking the governor's daughter against her will?"

"I was in the grog shop on the night with LaFoote, sure, but that's only because I was trying to save Rebecca, not kidnap her."

"And yet here you are without so much as a scratch on you. Strange that others who crossed paths with LaFoote did not fare as well."

"I had something he wanted. We made a deal, LaFoote and me."

The commodore chimed in. "Is that how you came to be in command of his ship? By throwing in your lot with that vile LaFoote?"

William Shakespeare was right: there would be no justice in *Black Spot's* court.

"I stole LaFoote's ship, that's all."

"So, you admit to being a pirate and a thief." This was still the commodore asking me questions. "And the squire? Did you murder him, too?"

I was speechless. The only way he could have known about the death of Rebecca's uncle was if she told him. Really, my trial could not have been going much worse.

"LaFoote killed the Squire. I watched him, but there was nothing I could do to prevent it."

"Nothing you could do or would do?" Before I could answer, he waved off my reply. "Makes no difference. Members of the jury, are you prepared to render a verdict?"

"We are."

"And what say you?"

The foreman stood. "On the charges of kidnapping, piracy, assault of a British merchant vessel, causing destruction, mayhem, and generally acting in a treacherous and treasonous manner, we find the defendant ..."

"If I may speak boldly, Your Most Pompous Papacy ..." It was William Shakespeare once more interrupting the proceedings. "Should thou not at least allow the lad a chance to explain his reasons for sailing before the mast of a pirate ship?"

The commodore eyed my scribe with disapproval. "Sounds to me as though you are sounding the depths of your own defense."

"Aye, the lad's case does have some bearing on the course I shall steer, but any defendant, especially one as special as this one, deserves to be heard."

"Special? In what way?"

"Speaks of treasure, he does, and lots of it."

"Treasure, you say?" Commodore Spotswood rubbed his chin thoughtfully. "Very well. I'll give the defendant a bit of latitude. Not that I expect his words will alter the verdict."

"Tell him what thou told me about the dog," said William Shakespeare.

I did not want to go into how I had experienced an absence seizure, fallen into a creek and ended up in pirate land, so I simply said, "When I was aboard the *Black Avenger*, there was a doctor who examined Barnacle. That's this dog I found. The doctor showed me markings on the mutt's belly that Doc claimed are the longitude and latitude of an island with enough treasure hidden on it to build an armada of ships and rule the high seas from the Barbary Coast to the Carolinas."

"I seriously doubt that," scoffed the commodore.

"Oh, the lad speaks the truth, Your Diminutive Dignitary. I've heard others tell of such treasure. Blood gold, they call it. Bought with the lives of those who traded their souls for worldly wealth."

"This treasure, you know its location?" asked the commodore.

"Not exactly, but I have a general idea of how to find it."

"And could sail there if necessary?"

"Yes sir, I believe I could."

"A delicious tale," the crown prosecutor said, "and so riddled with lies that it hardly holds a breeze. Sir, it is obvious the defendant is merely trying to save his own neck by concocting this outlandish story whereby he alone is the only one able to find this alleged treasure."

"I agree," said the commodore. "Why, not two weeks ago the pirate Pickled Pete stood before us with a similar account of some mysterious treasure that only he could locate. I think we've heard all we need to hear. Would the jury please render its verdict?"

"Having carefully considered all the facts, including the testimony of a convicted pirate, and given the fact that the defendant confessed to taking a pirate's ship and thus that makes him a pirate, we find the accused, Ricky Bradshaw ... guilty of piracy."

"Very well. Ricky Bradshaw," said the commodore. "Inasmuch as you have been found guilty of piracy, the penalty for which is death, it is the judgment of this tribunal that you are to be hanged by the neck until dead. May God Almighty have mercy on your soul."

The gavel struck.

The drum roll began.

"A final word with the lad, if I may."

"Make it quick," said the commodore, obviously irritated by the interruption.

"Did I not warn that thou wouldst not find justice in Black Spot's court? No and none ever shall. Treachery is his way." William Shakespeare bent closer, whispering, "Cheat the hangman and live to sail another day. That be the course thou should chart, now. Do that and thou might yet live to meet thy father."

I quickly glanced around at soldiers straining to hear us. "And how exactly do I go about doing that?"

"I know some chaps aboard the *Flying Dutchman* who would be mighty pleased to make your acquaintance. Just give a nod and I'll put in a good word for you with the Sergeant of Arms. Only, do not get caught in the *in between*?"

"What's the *in between*?"

"TIME'S UP!"

A moment later, I found myself standing on the gallows with a noose dangling over my head. In the distance, ships lay at anchor in the harbor. Nearby, waves crash against rocks, sending a shudder through the gallows' platform. A space of about three feet separated me from the fort's parapet. Three feet. The distance from the free-throw line to a basketball basket is fifteen feet and some NBA players can launch and dunk from there.

The hangman unfolded a hood to be placed over my head. Far away, a soldier coughed. Gulls screeched. I licked perspiration from my upper lip. I thought back to the way Greaves and Pugh had looked when they dropped, and I wanted no part of that, so …

Without a plan, without anything more than blind hope, I did my best Michael Jordan running-jump-at-the-free-throw-line-and-dunk-the-ball jump and … face planted into the wall.

"SHOOT HIM!"

Toes found a foothold. I climbed up, over and rolled onto my stomach, keeping low to avoid the volley of musket balls peppering the stonewall and flying over my head. Standing wasn't an option; kneeling wasn't an option. Staying on the top of the wall was not an option.

I rolled and rolled and … rolled off the high fort's wall.

You remember that scene in *Pirates of the Caribbean* where Jack Sparrow is led to the gallows to be hanged for piracy, and he dives into the sea to escape aboard the *Black Pearl*?

My landing did not end as well.

CHAPTER THREE

Caught in the In Between

They say hell is hot. Death Valley Desert hot. Steamy stifling hot, the way two-a-day football practices can be in August at Quiet High. Not that I would know anything about playing football. I'm not built for it. Plus, I don't like large, sweaty men lying on top of me. But I gradually became aware of a suffocating, sweltering heat and for a few minutes, I thought maybe I'd misjudged those television preachers who claim that hell is a percolating pond filled with fiery brimstone and deflated pool floats where sinners beg for mercy and a sip of cool water.

The one time I asked Mom about heaven and hell and what happens after we die, she tried to change the subject. We were in the carpool line outside the YMCA. My basketball coach had chewed me out pretty good during practice. Kept yelling for me to get back on defense, even though I was already beating the rest of my squad down the court. I was sitting in the passenger seat of Mom's KIA, listening to her while she went on and on about how I needed to get my grades up.

"You're starting on your homework first thing when you get home, young man. No watching soccer on your smartphone, do you understand?"

"Right, Mom. Because FIFA is the reason I'm struggling with negative infinity numbers."

"Don't get smart with me."

"But I thought you wanted me to get smart."

"Watch it, young man."

We rode in silence for a few moments and then I said, "Bet you wouldn't care about my grades so much if I was dead."

"Ricky!"

"Just saying, there are worse things than flunking algebra."

Mom rolled through a stop sign and pulled right out in front of a school bus. "Don't tell me you failed your midterm," she said, ignoring the bus's blaring horn.

"Okay, I won't."

"Are you serious?"

"It was a high F, Mom. Almost a D." Before she could yell at me some more, I said, "It's just that there's this kid who transferred into some of my class. He's been homeschooled. And he won't shut up about how I'm going to hell if I don't believe in Jesus."

"Don't use that word."

"Jesus?"

"You know what word I'm talking about."

"Is hell where Dad went when he died? I remember one time hearing you two arguing. You told Dad to go … there, and then not long afterward, he moved out and got killed in that truck crash."

Mom hit the blinker and aimed her KIA for the off-ramp to the mall. She shops when she's upset. Not that she buys stuff. That would cost money, and we're like, broke all the time.

"Tell me about basketball practice. Have they made you starting point guard yet?"

"You said I was a preemie, that I almost didn't make it. Would I have gone to hell?"

"I really wish you would stop saying that word." She turned into the mall parking lot. "Babies go to heaven, Ricky. I'm sure of it. Want to run into Whalebone's and take a look at those skater shoes you have on your Christmas list?"

"How about when I was six and ran into the street to get my basketball, and Mr. Wilson almost ran over me? What if I'd died then? Is that where I'd have gone?"

"Whalebone's it is."

"Come on, Mom. I'm serious."

"Boys in first grade go to heaven, Ricky. I'm sure of it. Now can we please talk about something else?"

"What about in seventh grade when that kid brought his dad's Glock to school and shot up the porta-johns beside the baseball field? What if I'd been in one of them and died?"

The light turned, and Mom gunned it, shooting across the intersection and into the mall parking lot. "Are you depressed? Having girl problems? I can make you an appointment if—"

"Mom, it's nothing like that. I told you, it's that homeschool kid. He won't shut up about Jesus."

Mom looked over at me. "I'm sure he means well, Ricky. When I was your age, I went through a phase like that."

"What kind of phase?"

"Handing out flyers, putting religious tracts on windshields. Once, I even protested outside an abortion clinic."

"You did? How come you're not like that now?"

"I grew out of it."

"But we still go to church. I mean, not regular, but sometimes, like on Easter and Christmas."

Mom parked the car and turned the engine off. "I didn't say I grew all the way out of it." She reached over and rested her hand on my shoulder. "Your dad's in a better place. We all end up in a better place."

But now I wasn't so sure. I was thinking maybe Mom was wrong about heaven and hell and that maybe the boy in my class was right: maybe there is a God. And if there is, I had a feeling I'd ended up in the bad place where it's hot all the time.

"Rick ... he. Rick ... he."

I heard the voice but couldn't tell if it's far off, close by, or in my head. But the place where I was, was definitely hot.

"If toucan hear me, wheeze Thailand." I made a fist.

"Good, Ricky, berry good. I'd still like to run some tests," the voice said. "See if there's any neurological damage."

"But he's okay, right?"

Another voice, I thought. *Female, familiar.*

"He appears to be fine, but I won't know for sure until I see his results. In the meantime, try not to get your son too excited, okay? We don't want to trigger another episode."

The bong of a hospital intercom came from right over my head. Close by came the clatter of a cart rolling down a hallway.

"Ricky? Ricky, honey, can you hear me?"

You know how you feel in the morning when the alarm goes off, and all you want to do is stay under the covers and sleep? How you know if you don't get up you'll be late for school, but instead of opening your eyes, you burrow your head under the pillow and wish with all your might that it's Saturday and not Monday. You know that feeling?

That's how I felt⎯like I was dead to the world.

"I'm here, sweetie, it's okay."

The woman's words drew me fully awake. I opened my eyes. From the cart's clattering wheels, and intercom bong and chirping of machines, I expected to find myself lying in a hospital bed. Back when I'd fallen into the creek the night my absence seizure started, I had momentarily seen myself lying on the dock with EMTs working on me. It was like some out of body experience. I'd never been sure if that really had happened or it was only in my head.

Now I thought the EMTs had actually rushed me to the hospital. But that's not what I found when I opened my eyes. When I opened my eyes, I saw that I most definitely was not in a hospital.

Instead, I stood in one corner of a small hut with a thatched roof and bamboo walls. The woman was kneeling on the sand a few feet in front of me. She wore a white turtleneck under a blue sweater, and her hair was tucked into a bun. Leaning over a rickety cot, the hem of her skirt barely touched the backs of her calves. I could not see the face of the person leaning beside the cot, but I knew it was Mom. She'd worn that dress the day we'd gone to the mall and talked about hell.

"How you doing, baby, you feeling okay?" She was speaking to the person on the cot. It was like she didn't even know I was standing behind her. I tried to answer, but no words came out. No words from me, anyway. The body on the cot, though, that person groaned.

Mom lost it. She hugged the person so tightly I thought she might break a rib. But here's what's weird: I could feel her squeezing. And it felt good. After several moments of sobbing and sniffling, she pulled a tissue from her skirt pocket and dabbed her eyes. As she did, I got a good look at the body.

The body was me, and I did not look so good. I had cuts on my chest, face, and arms, and my skin was a ghastly pale gray. Only then did I realize that I could not see myself standing in the hut. No feet, no legs, nothing. I was an invisible spirit.

To be honest, I kind of wanted to run away and cry. Except without legs, it was, you know, hard to run.

"Ricky, honey, is there anything I can get for you?" Mom was back to talking to the body of me on the cot. Standing where I was as a spirit I tried to answer but could not make a sound.

My body answered with a raspy, croaking, "Water."

Mom dipped a ladle into the wooden bucket next to her and scooped, lifted my head with her free hand, and pressed the ladle to my lips. I felt its refreshing wetness fill my mouth; I tasted its lukewarm sweetness. A little dribbled down my body's chin. Mom mopped it up with her tissue.

You know what's weird? What's weird is getting picked up by the pirate police and getting shipped off to Port Charles to stand trial for piracy and then getting accused of stealing a pirate ship, kidnapping a governor's daughter, explaining to the judge that you may in fact be dead, and being sentenced to hang, then getting warned twice by some guy named William Shakespeare to *cheat the hangman* and steal away on a ship sailed by the dead and doomed, jumping from the gallows and fort and ending up in a hut on a beach with your body on a cot and your mother tending to it. That's what's weird.

"As soon as the doctor says it's okay for you to travel, we're moving as far away from here as possible. I've already spoken with a trucking company based in Kansas City. They're holding a position for me."

"The Royals are ... the worst." This was my body's feeble attempt at a joke. Mom fed it another gulp of water.

I wonder if this is what William Shakespeare meant when he warned against getting caught in the between.

Looking in my direction, my body replied, "I don't think that's what he meant at all."

You heard that?

"Of course."

"Ricky, honey, who are you talking to?"

"Nobody, Mom. No *body* at all."

Ha, ha. Very funny.

My body shifted its gaze back to Mom. "Any visitors?"

"I've been checking your cell. You're getting texts from friends saying they want to stop by and visit. But it's Christmas, you know, and a lot of them are out of town or with their family."

Really? Still? Feels like I've been in pirate land for weeks.

"I thought I saw Becky Nance on the dock," my body said.

"She's one of those who texted. Was asking about some study notes."

Figures.

"Had another seizure, didn't I?" My body's voice was losing some of its hoarseness.

"Please, I'd rather we discuss all this when your doctor is here."

"Must've been a bad one."

"Please, can we talk about something else?"

"How long was I in the creek, Mom?"

Mom thumbed bangs away from my eyes and sighed heavily. "My dispatcher called me last night not long after you and I talked on the phone. He said something bad had happened, and I needed to get home. But with it being Christmas Eve and me in Memphis, there was no chance at all getting a flight home. Not that I could have afforded one, anyway. A receiving clerk on the loading docks overheard me talking on my cell and offered to call his brother-in-law who is a private pilot. Hour and a half later, we were in the air. A sheriff's deputy met me at the Williamsburg airport and drove me straight here. I haven't even bothered to go see what's left of our apartment." She gestured toward a stump in a corner of the hut. "I've been in that chair the whole time, waiting for you to snap out of it."

"More water."

"Careful, Ricky. I don't want you to drink too much too fast."

"Don't care. I'm dying of thirst."

I wasn't sure if that was meant to be a joke or not, but my body winked at me.

"Hey, I almost forgot." She reached into her purse and rummaged around. "Bought this on my way into Memphis."

Mom pulled a snow globe out of a gift bag and shook it. "Elvis told me to tell you hello."

Even though I was several feet away from the cot, I could tell the snow globe was a miniature replica of Graceland. A plastic figurine of Elvis Presley stood on the front porch. The King was wearing white bell-bottom pants, a sequin shirt open to the waist, and a wide black belt with gold buckles. His shiny coal-black hair was slicked back, showing off fat sideburns.

"If it's okay with you, I'm going to run down to the cafeteria. I haven't eaten anything since last night. Okay if I leave?"

"Go. I'll be fine."

"If you start feeling sick or woozy, press that button. The nurse's station is right outside your door."

I looked to where she pointed, but all I saw was a bamboo door and a sliver of beach and palms beyond. Mom kissed me on the forehead.

Once she was gone, me on the cot glanced over to where I stood and said, "Boy, that was close. Thought for sure she was going to turn around and see you."

Maybe she can't.

"Well, I sure can. You're like a faint shadow. Is that a hockey stick on the wall behind you?"

I peer over my shoulder. *Spear.*

"You sure? Looks like a hockey stick from here." My body tilted the snow globe, examining it. "Who's this with Elvis? I can't make them out."

I float over. *His manager, Colonel Tom Parker. Woman beside Parker is Priscilla.*

"And the little guy peeping out the window?"

Ed Sullivan.

"Awesome. I know we give Mom a hard time about buying shakers for us, but this is a good one. The first in our new collection."

Us? We're the same, you dork. There is no "we" or "us."

"Doesn't feel that way. Feels like we're drifting apart. It's like I don't even know who you are anymore."

Stop making jokes and get up. We need to get going.

"Go where?"

Wherever William Shakespeare is. Maybe he can explain how to put us back together.

"You mean like couples therapy? Forget it. This is my chance to start over, to be my own person. I'm tired of you running my life for me."

This is odd, me arguing with myself. I wonder if this is what William Shakespeare meant about getting caught in the "in between."

"Doubt it. I think it's something else."

Come on, on your feet. We need to get out of here before Mom comes back.

"No way. I'm not budging. Now that I'm back home, I'm staying put."

You're not home. You're in a hut on a beach.

My body tucked the snow globe under his left thigh and pointed at the wooden water bucket. "Says Sentara Williamsburg Regional Medical Center on that water pitcher. That's home enough for me."

I examined my surroundings more closely. Cot, sand, hut, spear on the wall, thatched roof. Nearby came the sound of surf slapping sand. Gulls squawked. The hut did not look anything like a hospital room.

"Check the medical chart hanging on the door," my body said. "Or ask one of those nurses outside my room."

This is bad. Really bad.

"Maybe you can find a spooky castle to haunt."

Shut up.

"You shut up."

Up, we're leaving.

My body folded its arms over its chest. "Nope. Staying right here."

Don't you want to find Dad? See if what they say about him is true?

"Nope. Mom loves me. Dad left. Far as I'm concerned, he can stay dead and gone."

Momma's boy.

"Maybe, but I'm alive, and you're not. Besides, I don't believe a single word of what William Shakespeare said. No way he's the famous playwright from England. Bet he made up all that stuff about the *Flying Dutchman,* too."

But what if he didn't? Wouldn't you like to see Dad one more time?

"All I want to do is get out of this hospital."

I'm going to find Dad. Or at least try.

"Good luck with that."

Come on, get up.

"No."

Up!

"Nuh-uh."

Look, if you don't—

WHAP!

A shirtless man wearing a butcher's apron advertising EARL THE BUTCHER'S BUTCHER SHOP barged into the hut. He had on grubby black boots, dirty pants, and held a meat cleaver in his fat fist. Furry muttonchops covered chubby cheeks; large tufts of hair sprouted from armpits. In smaller letters beneath the shop name were the words: REPLACEMENT PARTS FOR ALL MAKES AND MODELS.

The enormous man bent over my body and crinkled his nose. "Whoo-wee. Good thing I got here when I did. Few more minutes in this heat, and the cargo woulda turned rancid fer sure."

Cargo?

The butcher poked and prodded my body with the edge of his cleaver, mumbling under his breath, "Need a bit of work, this one does, no doubt about it. Can't put something like this up for auction, no sir."

Auction? What auction?

"Made a deal, didn' ya? Swapped yer body fer sump'n. I ferget what. Got paperwork here somewhere." Earl the Butcher reached into the front pouch of his apron.

As he did, I got a fresh look at my body. It did not look good. My skin was grayer than before, eyelids frozen in the half-shuttered look of the dead.

I didn't make any deal.

"Sure you did. Hang on, it's here someplace."

From the front pocket of his apron, he pulled an assortment of body parts: a thumb, a toe, a fistful of teeth … a mangled ear. "Ah, here 'tis." He unfolded a crumpled piece of paper and started reading loudly. "To tha person or persons in possession of said cargo, be it hereby resolved this stiff's soul has released all rights to the Sergeant of Arms aboard the *Flying Dutchman* in exchange fer … and then I can't read the rest. Too much blood on it."

Sergeant of Arms? Flying Dutchman? I never signed any agreement.

"Says here ye did. See?" He shoved the crumpled paper at me.

I examined the signature. *That's an X. Anybody could've put that there.*

"Got a dispute with yer contract, ye need ter take it up with the legal department. I'm jest in charge of shipping."

Wait a sec, you can hear me?

"'Course I kin. Whaddye think? I'm deaf and blind?" He stuffed my so-called contract back in his apron and leaned out the doorway. "Snake, Clean Willie? Get in here. We got a cool one that needs boxing up."

Two men, both filthy and unshaven, pushed their way into the hut. The shorter of the two held a bloody boar by its hind leg.

"I apologize fer us not getting here sooner," Earl the Butcher said, "but we was running a little behind." He gestured toward the boar's butt. "Get it? Running a little behind . . . Never mind. Snake, grab the head end of the cot." The taller of the two men, a lanky fellow with a bulging Adam's apple, looked nervously at my body. "Clean Willie, you get tha feet. An' careful you don' drop the cargo like ye did the last load. Like ter never got that feller put back together."

"Got it, boss. Get a grip and get'r done."

"Shut up, Snake."

"Aye, aye, boss."

"I said stop talking!"

"No, you said shut up."

Earl the Butcher whacked the tall man on the back of the head.

Hold up! Where are you taking me?

"To the *Dutchman* like I told ya. We're due ter sail at nine bells. Or maybe it's twelve. Numbers ain't my specialty. Digits is. See?" Earl the Butcher produced a handful of fingers and toes from his apron.

But you can't take my body. That's kidnapping!

"First off, ye ain't a kid no more. Stopped being one of them when ye sprouted whiskers on yer chin. Second, every soul says the same thing. Do anything ta keep from dying, they will. Lie, steal, beg. Or in yer case, cheat the hangman. Then when it's time to pay the pauper, they complain 'bout the terms. Take ye I can and will. Turtle Bill of late'n says so."

"Ah, boss? We got company."

I don't care what your sheet of paper says, it's MY body we're talking about.

"I mean it, boss, you need to take a look."

"Can't you see I'm busy, here?"

"But it's them cannibals. They're headed this way."

"Cannibals?" Earl the Butcher hurried to where Snake stood peeking out the bamboo door. "Blimey! Them headhunters will be none too happy 'bout us taking thar lunch." Earl pivoted back toward the shorter man who still clutched the curly tail of the bloody boar's butt. "Clean Willie, toss that thing on tha cot and pick up yer end. Snake, stop gawking at them pygmies and get ter work. We'll go out the back door."

"But, boss, there ain't no back door."

With his meat cleaver, Earl the Butcher hacked away at the bamboo wall and made a large hole. "DOOR!" Both men rushed through the ragged hole at the same time. "Tha cargo, ya imbeciles! Fetch tha cargo!"

The two grubby pallbearers snatched my body and went trotting away with Earl the Butcher close behind. He'd only gone a few steps before he stopped, whirled, and said to me, "You coming?"

Coming where?

"Ter see yer pop. He's dying ter meet ya. Or could be, he already has."

CHAPTER FOUR

Out-of-Body Experience

Around the age of twelve, I had a cavity filled by our family dentist, a man named Dr. Wu. Dr. Wu gave me a shot of Novocain to numb my gum, but it didn't help. As soon as he began drilling for oil in my skull, I bucked in the chair. Dr. Wu seemed surprised by my reaction: acted like it had never occurred to him that having a sharp and hard, object jabbed into a hole with raw nerve endings might hurt. Sighing, he placed his drill back on the metal instrument tray, left the room, and returned a few minutes later with Mom. She signed a form giving Dr. Wu permission to use nitrous oxide on me, then an assistant put the mask over my nose and mouth and told me to breathe normally.

I did and promptly floated up to the ceiling where I hung out for the duration of the excavation.

For the next few minutes, I had the impression that I was looking down on myself sprawled in the chair, slobbering and bleeding, but otherwise not really minding the procedure at all. The drill bit ground pulp and rotten tooth and sent smoke or dust upwards, but I didn't mind. Far as I was concerned, Dr. Wu could have chopped off my head and I wouldn't have cared. That's how I felt as I watched the two men carry my body on the cot through the jungle. It was like I was having an out- of-body experience fueled by nitrous oxide.

Snake and Clean Willie tromped through underbrush and splashed across small creeks, all the while grumbling about the heat and stickiness of the tangled underbrush. Earl the Butcher led the way, slashing and hacking with his meat cleaver through vines and green fronds that grew thick as kudzu. My lifeless hands and feet flopped about as the pair jostled my body. Carrion flies, those gross insects that lay eggs in decaying flesh, buzzed in and out of my body's mouth and nose. It was clear to all, me especially, that I was dead. What I couldn't figure out was why my spirit or soul or whatever, could still see myself dead.

It's like I'm stuck between heaven and hell.

As soon as I thought this, Snake cocked his head and said, "Prayed, didn't you?" Sort of winking, he added, "Asked for help?"

Wasn't exactly a prayer. I mean, not really because I'm not sure I believe in God.

"A body sees the things I've seen and you'll get a whole different perspective on The Big Guy."

"No talking to the cargo!" Earl the Butcher's fat fist caught Snake square on the side of the man's head. "Talking to the cargo be a code violation!"

"Sorry, boss."

There's a code?

"'Course thar's a code. And a union and dues and everything. Though ah admit that lately, tha head of our union ain't been bargaining in good faith."

What sort of union could you possibly be a member of?

"The Able Bodied Alliance of Body Snatchers. Head of my local, I am. Get it? Head of my …"

"Hey, that's a good one, boss," said Snake.

WHACK! "For the love of Louie Lou Eye would you *please* shut up?"

"Aye, aye, boss."

"Had a patch on ma apron ta prove it, but it fell off," Earl the Butcher said.

"Tell him about the strike!"

"Told ya ta keep quiet."

"No you didn't, boss, you said …"

"Snake, I swear," Clean Willie said, "you got the brains of a coral reef."

While Snake scowled at Clean Willie Earl said, "A few months back, membership voted to go on strike due to poor working conditions. Lack of bathroom breaks, low wages, no vacation, or sick days. Eternity is a long time to go without a potty break. Management warned us they'd dissolve our union if we didn't call off tha strike. Said they would and could and did. Now I'm what cha might call a scab. Haul cargo like yours an' such ta make ends meet. Get it? Make ends meet … I'm a scab …"

If you're trying to be funny, you're playing to a dead crowd.

"Hey, boss. The corpse made a funny."

"Snake, I swear, if you don't …

Am I an able body?

"Can't say. That's up to the Sergeant of Arms of the *Flying Dutchman*. At least yer in one piece; that's a good sign. Some loads we get is so disjointed I can't make heads nor tails of which end is up. An' even when a body is all in one piece, like yourn, some is so mangled and cut up that it takes nearly a week ta stitch 'em back together. Can'y make no money on that sort of cargo. Speaking of good signs, I'm supposed to give ya a talisman."

A what?

"Talisman. It's like a lucky rabbit's foot only different. All tomb raiders gets one."

Who said anything about tomb raiders?

"I did, didn' ya hear me? Snake, remind me to have tha cargo's hearing checked before we ship him aboard. Might have a bit o' seaweed lodged in his ears."

My basketball coach says people make their own luck.

"Ya might think about changing yer recipe. Don't look like it's working so good for ya. Talisman might help. It's a long an' dangerous voyage yer undertaking. Be dragons and sea monsters out there."

Sea monsters? Really?

"Could be it's more along tha lines of Williams and shipwrecks and coral reefs so sharp they'll cut ya ta shreds. If you're hoping ter find your pop, you'll be needin' all the help ya can get."

Who said anything about me trying to find Dad?

"I did, just then. Swear ta goodness yer deaf as a headstone. Boys yer age is always curious 'bout their pop. Wants tar know if he got intar any scrapes, had girlfriends, stole stuff. That sort of thing. Sides, you need tar find him so you can kill 'm."

Why would I want to kill Dad?

"To show him ya's big and tough and can run things on your own. Or run 'em inter tha ground. Seen that happen, too."

Dad's dead so that's not going to happen.

"Thing ter keep in mind, is that tha dead don' stay dead. Says so in the Bible. Forget where. Saw a verse penned to tha shirt of a sailor. Print was all smudged on account of he was a drowner, like you. But I'm not supposed ter be talking ter ya 'bout this."

Because it's against the code.

"'Zactly."

To be honest, his comment about me being a drowner bothered me. A lot, actually. It sort of confirmed what I suspected happened when I had the seizure on the dock and seemed to come out of it, but maybe didn't come out of it all the way and ended up on the dock with paramedics trying to resuscitate me.

Our walk through the jungle ended at the edge of a sweeping meadow. On the far side, beyond the cluster of ramshackle rooftops that marked the outskirts of a town, I could just make out a wide blue bay crowded with ships. Earl and his men, carrying my cot, crossed the field and headed down an alleyway that led us through the business district where sailors gathered in the doorways of grog shops. Earl's men halted at a low seawall that separated the waterfront's cobblestone street from the beach and bay.

"Take a load off, boys. Appears our ship ain't come in yet."

Snake and Clean Willie dropped the cot on the beach-side of the seawall. I guess this was to keep nosey pedestrians from asking questions. A rattling, gasping gurgle escaped from my corpse's mouth. Lips had begun to recede, exposing the tops of pinkish-gray gums.

"Snake, I'm putting ya in charge of tha cargo," Earl said. "Anything happens, it's coming outta yer salary."

Snake made a face as if he'd bitten into a rancid prune. "But I don't get a salary, boss."

"And you won't get none neither if you don't hush your bellyaching. Want me ter call the temp service? Tell 'em to send a replacement?"

"No, boss! I wasn't bellyaching, honest."

Earl looked in my direction and said in a hushed tone like we were sharing a secret, "A soul gets mighty desperate when they got nothing ter do fer days on end except treed water in a fiery lake. Few centuries of that and a feller will do most anything ter get a shot at real work."

So Snake and Clean Willie are ... I was going to go with "dead" but Earl interrupted my thought.

"My regular crew? Not hardly. They's just a couple of stiffs I picked up at the day laborer lot."

"Where you going, boss?"

"To see a man about a dog."

"A dog? What sort?"

Covering his face with his hands, Earl shook his head as if he wished to strangle Snake.

"What about that thing you were supposed to give me?"

"Tha talisman." Frowning, Earl the Butcher scanned the waterfront street, then shrugged. "I'm sure it'll show up. At least you better hope it does. Lots of dangers ahead where yer going."

What sort of dangers?

"Hard to say. Different for each soul. Marauding pirates, worms tha size of yer fingers, rats big as yer arm. Squalls and shipwrecks and boiling hot days adrift at sea ... coral reefs sharper than a dirk and tombs filled with treasure and dead men's bones. It's all in the book."

What book?

"The one you don' got yet." Earl looked sternly at Snake. "Keep an eye on the cargo. Slippery one, he is. Might try'n sneak off. Lose tha cargo and heads 'ill roll, understand?"

"I'll do my best."

"That's what I'm afraid of," Earl mumbled.

I watched Earl the Butcher stride across the street and enter a pub.

"Should've let me go with him," Snake said under his breath. "I could've helped him find that man's dog."

"Boss ain't going to find no dog, you idiot. He's got a date with a lady friend."

"Don't call me an idiot."

"Then stop acting stupid."

"And don't call me stupid."

"Help swat them flies buzzing over the cargo," Clean Willie said. "Can't have 'em laying eggs in the cargo's nose."

"I'm not stupid," Snake grumbled.

"Are too."

"Am not."

You want to go see a man about a dog? Help me help you.

"Help you how?" Snake asked.

"Bad idea, Snake. Boss warned you about talking to the cargo."

"Who's talking? I'm just listening." Snake pivoted to cut Clean Willie out of the conversation. "I never had a dog, but I always wanted one."

So I find you a dog, and you help me. We got a deal?

Snake nodded.

The beach along the waterfront was a mess. Men lounged about among the piles of garbage, heaps of palm branches piled into kindling for campfires, and makeshift tents. I was hoping to see a stray mutt or some other dog I could pretend to give to Snake. My thinking was that if I could ... Okay, I wasn't really sure what I was thinking. My body was dead, and apparently, I was only a spirit floating between two dead men. But I had to try something. Earl the Butcher seemed deadly serious about shipping my corpse onto the *Flying Dutchman* once it arrived—not that I seriously thought it would. I had made myself clear on that point. What I needed was a break, some good luck. *Or maybe a good luck charm.* No sooner had the thought left my mind when a dog came trotting toward us. And not just any dog, mind you, but one with curly black fur, pointy ears, and an all-to-familiar gait.

Barnacle!

The dog cocked its head. *It's me, Ricky. Here, boy.*

For a moment, it looked like the mutt would come over to where I was standing (floating, actually), but at the last

DEAD CALM, BONE DRY

moment, his ears stood up; he pivoted and went trotting into a place called The Blind Monkey.
　"Hold up! Where do you think *you're* going?" Snake asked me.
　To see a dog about a treasure.
　"Wait, I'm coming with you!"

CHAPTER FIVE

GOING TO SEE A DOG ABOUT A TREASURE

Snake caught up to me in the doorway of The Blind Monkey. A hand-painted sign propped against the doorframe advertised A FREE EAR PIERCING WITH THE PURCHASE OF A BOTTLE OF KILL DEVIL. I peered inside the darkened pub, searching for Barnacle while men inside, most of whom were unshaven and had their shirts open to the waist, leaned against ceiling supports or slouched in chairs. From all appearances, The Blind Monkey was a seething den of pirates, rascals, and drunken sailors ... and just the sort of place a salty dog would frequent.

"See him? Is my dog in there?"

Too dark to tell. And it's not your dog. Not yet, anyway.

Here and there, I caught snatches of arguments laced with cursing. Mugs clanked as crewmates boasted of past voyages and the ones to come. The tavern smelled of sour ale, sweat, and tobacco smoke.

I could go in and look, but there's too much smoke. I might get caught up in the haze and lose myself. But if I was back in my body, well then I could ...

"Sorry, mate. Can't help you there. Something like that is beyond my pay grade. 'Sides, company policy has a 'no refunds' on cargo wishing to back out of their deal. Cargo is to go aboard the *Flying Dutchman* complete and intact."

You and I both know there's no such ship.

"Hush your mouth! Crew of the *Dutchman* get powerful upset when a soul speaks ill of them. Do things to folks, they do. Unspeakable things. Seen it happen. Seen worse than that, too."

What could be worse than having your body stolen and sold to a ship full of ghosts?

"Coming face-to-face with Neptune, Poseidon, and the souls of them from the lost city of Atlantis. Why, one time I even saw the dreaded Kracken."

Kracken?

"Only the most feared sea monster there is. Big as a ship. Been known to wrap its tentacles around vessels and pull whole vessels down to Davy Jones."

You've seen this happen?

"Not exactly. A Portuguese freighter I served on hauled part of the Kracken's tentacle aboard. Dreadful stench. Ran the length of the deck, it did. Was big around as the main mast with suckers the size of my foot and sharp as a dirk. Seeing a thing like that will make you think twice about going to sea again."

All this talk of sea monsters sounded interesting, but at any moment, Earl the Butcher could return, and I would lose what small chance I had to get back my body. *A few minutes ago, your* boss hinted that you were like me. A lost soul. How is it you still have such a nice body?

"What? This old thing?" Snake tucked one muddy foot behind the other. "Nothing more than a hand-me-down. Boss picked it up at MacGyver's Cadaver Paint and Body Shop. Original owner was a pastor, and when he gave up the ghost, he headed the other direction, if you know what I mean. Just goes to show, you never know about folks and what's in their dark souls." Snake pointed to a place on his elbow where a bone poked through his thin skin. "You can see where it's worn out, some."

Would you like a newer, nicer model? Something with less mileage on it?

"Nicer body? You bet!"

Give me mine back, and I'll pay you enough to get a top-of-the-line model.

"Wish I could, but rules are rules."

I'll give you some gold. Enough for you to get a new suit of clothes for the new body you're going to buy. And maybe enough for a bath and shave?

Snake cast a sideways glance across the street at Clean Willie, who sat on the seawall, his muddy feet resting on my corpse. "I, ah … better not."

How about a pair of shoes to go with your new body and outfit? Something with good leather on the bottoms?

Snake eyed his muddy feet. "A pair of new work boots wouldn't be so bad. Hurts something awful walking on coral and lava rock with just my bare feet. Only thing boss man pays me is no mind."

Check out the gold in my pocket. Decide for yourself if it's the real deal or not. What could it hurt?

He scrunched his face as if deep in thought. "I guess there wouldn't be any harm in at least looking."

I followed Snake back across the street (him walking, me floating). We stopped next to my body. With my eyes half-closed in a blank stare and purple lips curling back over dark gums, my corpse looked worse than dead. Made me want to barf. Except without a body, I couldn't.

Clean Willie paused from shooing flies from my mouth. "What are you doing, Snake?"

"Nothing."

"Doesn't look like nothing. Looks like you're talking with the cargo."

"Mind your own business."

"Didn't you learn your lesson the last time?"

Last time?

"Snake here got put in charge of robbing graves," Clean Willie said. "First offense, right?"

Snake cupped his hands over his ears. "Not listening."

"The undertaker had planted a fresh one that day. A barrister. Right then, Snake sees the man's spirit standing next to the gravesite, and so he asks the barrister if he's open to doing some legal work. Complains that he's got a dispute with the boss man. What was it you called it? Religious discrimination?"

Snake, with his eyes closed and hands still over his ears, replied, "My family is Protestant. Boss man is Irish Catholic. Claimed my background didn't have anything to do with me having to do all the digging, but I know otherwise."

"Anyways, boss man heard about Snake seeking legal counsel from the barrister and banished him to you know where for ... how long was it?"

"Nearly all the Dark Ages," Snake said sheepishly.

"That's how come I can't figure out why he's talking to the cargo when he knows what'll happen if he gets caught."

"See?" Snake said to me. "Told you this was a bad idea."

Just look in the front pocket of my trousers. If you don't like what you see, no worries.

"Guess there's no harm, really, in looking," he said mostly to himself, and then reached inside the front pocket of my cut-off jeans.

"Bad idea, Snake."

"Shut up."

"Don't say I didn't warn you." Clean Willie hopped off the seawall. "And you? You think getting back in your body will fix everything? Don't work like that. The men aboard the *Flying Dutchman*, they don't see cargo like yours every day. Young, fit, and with all its teeth. Body like yours without holes or broken bones is a prize for sure. Renege on your deal, and the crew of the *Flying Dutchman* will hunt you for all of eternity. Probably haunt you, too." Clean Willie picked up his dead pig by its hind legs. "See you in hell, Snake."

"Back atcha."

Snake waited until Clean Willie was out of sight before fishing around in the pants pocket. When he found the shiny medallion Rebecca returned to me, he grinned, revealing some serious dental decay.

"Wow, it's heavy. Must be worth a fortune."

Came from the Nuestra Señora De Riqueza. *At least that's what I was told.*

Snake studied the medallion as if mesmerized by its shiny appearance. "And I can keep it?"

If you give me back my body, yes.

"I can't show you how to put on the cargo," Snake said. "Boss man never explained that part to me."

As long as you say it's mine, that's good enough for me. I'll figure it out from there.

Snake rubbed his chin with the back of his fist. "Clean Willie is right about one thing: absconding with the cargo is risky business. It's one thing for a spirit to loiter about in graveyards scaring folks. It's something else altogether to walk in another person's shoes."

DEAD CALM, BONE DRY

Do we have a deal?

Snake looked nervously up and down the street, then closed his fist around the medallion. "Deal!"

The last I saw of Snake, he was sprinting up an alleyway toward a placed called The Body Shop.

The good news was, I was alone with my corpse, and no one seemed to notice or care.

Bad news was that right then a larger than normal wave rushed up the beach past the tide line, washed over the cot, rebounded off the seawall, and retreated ... taking my lifeless body with it.

CHAPTER SIX

THE MAN WITH THE EYE PATCH

When I finally caught up with my corpse floating face down in the water, it wasn't—floating, I mean. It had sank. *Or is it sunk?* Anyway, the cot was drifting away on a rip current, and my corpse was underwater and going down fast. I did the only thing I knew to do: I spirited myself into the murky blackness and embraced myself the best I could as a spirit. (Professional counselors recommend we do this even if we are generally upbeat and feel good about ourselves.) And guess what? It worked.

When I surfaced, a gruff-sounding man with a thick British accent was warning me that bathing with all my clothes on was not allowed. "And no loitering, neither. You want to sleep, do it elsewheres."

I was back in my skin. Funny how being true to yourself and not trying to be someone else can work wonders for a body.

I studied the cuts and bruises on my chest, arms, and legs. *Probably from the rocks and reef by the fort.* My head felt like it weighed fifty pounds. Salt burned the raw areas on my ankles and wrists where ropes and shackles had cut into my skin. My bindings were gone. I was a free man, a liberated pirate. For a few moments, I floated on my back, tolerating the sting of open wounds. Pain meant I was alive. Pain meant I survived my jump from the gallows. I took a deep breath, dove under, tossed my head back, and waded out. My legs were so rubbery I nearly face-planted on the sand.

In a dirt clearing across the street, vendors hawked bananas, conch, fish, and coconuts. Dogs fought; mothers yelled at toddlers playing in filthy piles of garbage. Not far from the open-air market, bare-chested men loitered in the doorway of The Blind Monkey. Faded pennants from European countries fluttered above its entrance. I pushed my way past the crowd blocking its doorway, apologizing and getting shoved back for my trouble. Candles flickered on tables. Swarthy men wearing cutlasses and knives and brandishing pistols let me know they were ready for a fight. Most had rings in their ears and bright scarves around their heads. If ever there was any doubt I was anywhere other than pirate land, those doubts vanished.

I admit: I was scared. Who wouldn't be? The pub was dark and ominous, a word here that means not-friendly-to-boys-from-Quiet-Cove-who-are-having-an-absence-seizure.

I kept my gaze aimed at the floor of large flat stones and tried not to make eye contact. A husky man with a crutch under one arm and beer breath cursed me: for what reason, I had no idea. Being alive, I guess. He gave me a hard shove in the back that sent me stumbling into a large, burly man. I apologized and moved on, all the while scanning the floor for that mangy mutt Barnacle. He was, after all, the key to my pirate adventure. On his belly was the longitude and latitude of some mysterious treasure that would change the course of history. Or at least make for a good story when I got back home. But I did not see a dog. All I saw were fat, grubby feet and fat, scuffed boots that I was sure contained grubby, smelly feet.

At that moment—as almost always happens in books and movies—a dark, furry blob shot past.

Crawling on my hands and knees, I hurried after the dark, furry blob. This took courage, not to mention a deep breath on my part. And that deep breath almost didn't last, but then I saw the dog. *Stupid dog,* I thought. *If it weren't for you I wouldn't be in this mess.* I hoped Barnacle couldn't read spirit thoughts.

"How you doing, fella? Missed you. Did you miss me?" I pulled the dog close and buried my face in his stinking wet fur, hugging him tightly.

"Well, ain't t-this a t-t-touching sight. If it ain't me old shipmate, D-D-Dick Bradshaw."

Strange how in a moment of fear you notice small details like the stub of two knuckles on a hand, the patch over an eye, and the halting voice of a murderous pirate. A flickering candle on the table illuminated the man's face. "Turtle Bill?"

"Called that by some. Called worse, too."

"What happened to your eye?"

With the back of a hand, he bumped up the brim of his tricorn hat and touched his forehead. "Courtesy of our friend, Captain LaFoote." A ragged scar began beneath Turtle Bill's mousy-gray bangs and extended downward, curving into a crescent that disappeared under a black eye patch. "S-seems our c-c-cap'n warn't tha fool I took him ter be. Lucky to escape with my life, was I."

He hoisted a mug of strong-smelling drink. "Here's ter old friends and new sails. May both hold a steady course." With his boot, he pushed a chair towards me. "Sit."

I declined, remaining where I stood. "You must want something pretty badly to use that dog to lure me into this pub. For a few minutes, I thought he was glad to see me."

DEAD CALM, BONE DRY

"Sit, boy." The barrel of a pistol poked over the edge of the table.

Reluctantly, I dropped into the chair across from him. Which, as you're about to find out, is how I got roped into going hunting for pirate treasure.

CHAPTER SEVEN

WE HATCH A PLAN TO STEAL A TREASURE

"Whatever it is you want, you can count me out. I'm done helping men like you."

"No need to be so standoffish, mate. We's crew. Share and share alike, thems are my stripes now."

I'll be honest: the haggard man seated across from me didn't look anything like the first mate I had served with aboard the *Black Avenger*. Back then, Turtle Bill had been so afraid of his shadow that every time the captain barked his name, he flinched. On board the ship his stuttering speech and diminutive stature made him the butt of jokes among the crew. But now, his grizzled appearance fit him perfectly: as long as he was a murdering pirate.

"I admit, I lived by my wits fer a time, that's a fact. But you see before you a reformed man, an honest seaman seeking fortune by fair means."

DEAD CALM, BONE DRY

"Men like you don't change."

"It's a fact, mate. I swear to Davy Jones' Locker. I'm done stealing and killing. Fair wages and fair seas, that's the life for me." He took another long gulp from his mug and wiped his mouth with the back of his sleeve. "What sort of deal did you make to get shed of the noose? I 'spect our friend Shaky fed ye a delicious tale 'bout cheating the hangman."

"Shaky?"

"William Shakespeare." He grinned. "Calls himself a playwright, he does. Shaky's good at making stuff up, I'll grant him that. But it's the demons in the bottle that gives him the shakes."

"So he's nothing more than a drunken sailor?" I said.

"Double-crossing pirate, he is."

I had been such an idiot. I knew William Shakespeare kept a bottle tucked in his frock. He even asked the commodore for rum at my trial. And still I'd sort of fallen for his tales.

"I never really believed he was the famous British playwright, but …"

"Playwright, my foot. Why, even with my one eye I could craft a better tale than that rascal. Gotter admit, though, he must've spun a good yarn ter get ye to escape the gallows."

"How come you're not on Coffin Cay? I would think by now you'd be digging for treasure."

Quick as a flash, Turtle Bill lunged across the table and clamped a hand on my arm. "Furl yer tongue, lad! You want ever' scoundrel in this pub knowing our business?"

"Our business? You must be kidding. No way I'm taking orders from a black-hearted, murdering thief like you."

At that moment, I heard myself, and I realized how stupid I sounded talking like a pirate.

"Don't be so quick ter strike yer colors. Leastways not 'til you've heard the terms of my offer."

"If it's stealing ships and killing crews, count me out."

"Aye, spoken like a lad who's served before the mast and lived to tell about it." He splashed more of the foul-smelling drink into his mug and said to me, "I'll allow I was mixed up with some cutthroats back aboard the *Avenger*. Be lying if I said otherwise. LaFoote's men would sooner stick a dirk in yer back than down a shot of rum, that's a fact. But I'm a reformed man now. No more bloodshed and thieving fer me."

"Yeah, right. You must be desperate if you're trying to get me to help."

Looking about as though someone might overhear us, Turtle Bill pulled a cloth map from his satchel. With great care, he smoothed the frayed edges so the map was flat on the table and motioned me closer toward the candle.

"This here's the course I sailed from Santa Maria." He traces a dotted line with his finger. "You kin see how I skirted the coast of Hispaniola and come up through the pass right there," he adds, thumping an X with his knuckle. "Then I drifted into the doldrums. Confounded heat ... no wind ... jellyfish so thick I couldn't even take a dip. Felt like the Devil's breath out there, it did. Lost my way. Nearly lost most of my mind, too. Got so blazing hot and still, I could hardly tell sky from sea. Fortunate I was ter finally catch a west-flowing current and fetch up here in Port Charles."

"Go on."

He took another gulp and wiped his whiskered lip with the back of his hand. "Had 'bout decided I'd ne'er find ... that island with tha treasure. Then I bumped into a boson's mate. Young feller, 'bout yer age. Crews on a Dutch frigate. Kept talking 'bout how his captain had plucked a boy from tha water not far from here. Lad was rumored to be tha skipper of a pirate ship. 'The *Black Avenger*,' says he. 'My luck has turned,' says I.'"

"Still don't understand why you need me. You have the dog. The coordinates for the island are tattooed on his belly. If you want to find Coffin ... that island, why not just sail there yourself? Why bring me into it?"

"Aye, thar's the rub. The dog here, he got inter a mess of fleas a ways back. Clawed and pawed his belly something awful. Now thar's nothing but scabs and scars where them digits was. Then there's this." Turtle Bill touched the black patch over his eye. "Down ter one eye. And that be my bad one. Makes it hard ter sight a sextant."

"Even if I knew how to find the island, why would I tell you? Why not just sail there myself?"

"Smart thinking, Dick. Figured once I told ye the lay of things, ye might angle ter cut old Turtle Bill out of his fair share. That's how come I secured a bit of leverage."

Turtle Bill shifted his gaze towards the bar area. As I pivoted in my chair, Rebecca came striding toward us from the shadows. My heart nearly leapt from my chest. (Lame thing to say, I know, but if it's possible to love someone born three hundred years ago, I am.) I couldn't believe it. After the trial, I thought I would never see her again.

She had changed from her white hoop dress into a long burgundy jacket with black lapels, a paisley print vest, and a ruffled shirt—baggy black pants, black boots, and brown felt hat with a feather tucked into its wide headband. She could have passed for a young sailor all decked out for a pending voyage if not for the rosy color of her cheeks.

Rebecca pulled a chair up to our table and straddled it. "Did he say yes?"

I pivoted from her to Turtle Bill. "What's she talking about?"

"Yer missy is asking if ye agreed ta serve as skipper on our voyage."

I looked at her. I was pretty sure even though this was a much nicer conversation than we had shared at my trial, it still would end up with me getting shot or hung. "He's kidding, right?"

Rebecca replied, "Does he appear to be kidding?"

"You're in on this, too?" She shrugged. Even shrugging, she looked hot, especially in her Penelope Cruz *Pirates of the Caribbean* outfit.

"That's just great. First the dog, now you? Is there not anyone who won't betray me?"

"I resent the accusation that the dog and I are equals," she said.

"Don' take it hard, mate. Share and share alike. That's the pirate code."

"She's not a pirate," I said. "And I'm not either."

"You would not know what I am. Or what I will and will not do," Rebecca shot back in an I'm-off-limits-to-you voice. "You have never stayed around long enough to find out."

"You two must be hard up if you're asking me for help, but that's fine. Doesn't bother me. But there's no guarantee I'll be able to remember those coordinates. I might just, you know, sail off the edge of this map. And if I do, you two will just have to accept that."

Turtle Bill offered his hand. "Do we have a deal?"

"What's in it for you?" I said to Rebecca. "I mean, back at the fort, you wanted me dead. Now you're ready to join me on a treasure. What's up with that?"

"Shiny objects," Turtle Bill explained on her behalf. "Girls always like things that glitter and shine."

"Seriously?"

"I have my reasons," Rebecca says, "and they do not concern you."

"So do we have an accord?" Turtle Bill asked, again.

I weighed my options. I had no illusions of what sort of disaster the trip would become. Turtle Bill couldn't be trusted to keep his word. He was a pirate, after all. Once he got the treasure—assuming there was a treasure to be got—he would probably put a musket ball in me. Maybe shoot Rebecca, too. But if I didn't help him, I was pretty sure Commodore Spotswood would find me, and then I would be worse off than before. The thing that really bothered me was why Rebecca. Knowing what she knew about Turtle Bill, we would be so eager to sail with such a thieving pirate.

"I'll sail you to that island if I can find it. But then I'm done helping you. And you," I said to Rebecca. "Hate me if you want for leaving you on that island with those freed Africans, but I do this, and we're even."

"That's the spirit, mate. All for one and none for all."

"So when do we sail?" Rebecca asked.

"Thar's the rub, mate. I'm in the market, as it were. Was hoping you would be so kind as to fetch us a vessel."

"You want me to steal a boat?"

"Blue one if you can," Rebecca added. "I have always wanted to own a blue boat."

"What happened to your ship?" I asked Turtle Bill.

"On yonder rocks by the harbor entrance." He touched his eye patch. "Like I's saying before. I'm down ter one eye and ..."

"It's your bad one, I know."

"So it's settled. Ye'll steal a ship and the missy and me 'ill meet ye off Rounder's Point at two bells."

"Wait? I have to do this by myself?"

"We got business to conclude, ain't that right?" Rebecca nodded, then winked at me.

I had no idea why or what she meant by the wink. If there was a grade for non-verbal communication skills with girls, mine would be an F.

"And mind yer not late. This place 'ill be crawling with British regulars once the commodore learns his fiancée has gone missing."

"You're ... engaged to Black Spot?"

"The commodore has asked fer yer missy's hand in marriage. Thought ye knew."

"Seriously?"

"But I have not given him my answer," Rebecca said to me. "I remain open to other proposals."

"Two bells, mate, and mind yer not late."

CHAPTER EIGHT

THE DEAD CALM, BONE DRY

I found Turtle Bill's gig right where he told me it would be. Back home, a gig is something the boys in my apartment complex use to spear frogs with, but in pirate land, it's a wooden boat that leaks. Turtle Bill's gig sat next to overturned fishing smacks on the beach not far from where the British soldier warned me to stop bathing in my clothes. I thanked the boy guarding the gig and gave him two guinea coins like Turtle Bill instructed. Here the word "instructed" doesn't necessarily mean "orders" because Turtle Bill's "instructions" were more along the lines of, "Go to the beach. Find my gig. If one of them boys asks ye fer money, push him aside and shove off. Them ruffians is always peddling fer change."

Giving the boy a few coins seemed like the least I could do. Besides, it wasn't my money. While searching for Barnacle in the grog shop I'd found the coins on the floor.

Paddling away from the beach I kept my head down. I didn't want any of the British soldiers to recognize me. As far as

DEAD CALM, BONE DRY

Commodore Spotswood was concerned, I was dead, so if word got back to the commodore that a shirtless male teen in cut-off jeans had washed up on the beach with rope burns on his wrists and ankles and then wandered away, he might come looking. And I definitely did not want to see him now that I knew he had proposed to Rebecca.

A white-hot sun burned my back. The echo of carriages rolling over cobblestone streets fell away. Only the slapping of my oars remained. I had no rosy illusions about what lay ahead. Helping Turtle Bill was stupid and dumb, but I couldn't see any other way off the island except to get a boat and sail away. Besides, there was the dog to think about. He was my only link to home and Quiet Cove, so the two of us had a bond of sorts. And there was the treasure on Coffin Cay to consider. Not that I expected we'd find any treasure if we actually reached Coffin Cay. But if I was going to steal a boat and not get caught, I needed a plan. Here was my plan.

Find the ugliest boat in the harbor and take that one. That was my plan.

And right then, all the way across the harbor, tucked up in a marshy area of the cove, I spied what had to be the ugliest ship ever built. She was tied to a drooping finger pier, and her hull was stained with salt and grime, making her look more gray than black. There were six gunports, all closed. Rotting ropes dangled from warped spreaders; dirty sails hung limp. A mossy beard of sea grass grew thick along her waterline. Judging from the vessel's untidy appearance, it was easy to imagine that she was riddled with Teredo navalis (Teredo worms), a species of saltwater clam (actually, marine bivalve mollusk, in case you're reading this book for biology lessons) within the Teredinidae family. According to some historical accounts, Teredo worms sank more pirate ships than all the guns in naval battles. Even Christopher Columbus had problems with them. On his fourth voyage to the Americas in 1502, all his ships sank because of worm damage.

I approached cautiously. Even an ugly, rotten boat might have its owner or crew aboard. But when no one appeared to wave me off, I tied off to her stern. It was then that I noticed the ship's name: *DEAD CALM*. The letters A in the words *DEAD* and *CALM* were painted to look like skulls. The other letters were painted like bones. To be honest, it looked pretty cool.

With fear and trepidation, I snuck aboard. *Trepidation*, by the way, is a word that was on my honors English midterm exam. It means a feeling of worry or agitation, a brooding sense something really bad may happen. That's exactly how I felt as I climbed up the back of the vessel: like something bad was about to happen. Of course, stealing the boat would make me exactly the thing I swore I would never become—a pirate. Then again, I was already labeled a pirate, so living up to my title seemed like the smart move.

Thing is, if you really want to do something badly enough, you can almost always talk yourself into it and justify what you want to do.

I swung my legs over the stern railing and dropped into a crouched position, scanned the deck quickly, then hurried toward the helm's station, ducking out of sight. I waited, listening and watching to see if anyone else was aboard. Finally, I spun the ship's wheel. There was resistance against the rudder, which was a good sign. At least the steerage system worked.

The deck was a mess. Ropes lay about uncoiled, and the rigging sagged from too little attention. I thumped the protective glass on the binnacle, and the gimbaled compass inside oscillated, pointing to true north. Steerage works, compass spins, mast is upright, sails are sort of okay … It wasn't much of a boat, but it was a boat. Best of all, it was blue.

I went below, exploring cabins and large rooms: closets and storage lockers. Eventually I worked my way into the galley, a fancy pirate word for ship's kitchen. Skillets and pots dangled by handles from support beams. A basket of rotten bananas sat on a rough-hewn wooden bench. Next to the bananas were a cutting board and meat cleaver. A kettle hung suspended over a smoldering fire. Chunks of meat and bits of carrots and green vegetables floated in gray, soupy chowder. Using a large ladle, I stirred the soup, then tasted. *Could use some pepper and salt,* I thought, *but it's not bad.* I dipped again and hooked a nice-size chunk of meat, leaned over and realized I'd snagged the . . . shriveled head of Snake.

Earl the Butcher had warned heads would roll if my body didn't make it aboard the *Flying Dutchman* and now one had.

"Ahoy, there! You with the gig, make yourself known!"

In case you're wondering, that's when the bad things I feared would happen . . . happened.

CHAPTER NINE

I STEAL A SHIP

"**B**oard that ship, men!" The command came so close I thought the individual was right next to me.

Snatching a meat cleave from its hook, I rushed back up top. By the time I reached the deck, British soldiers were charging up the boarding ramp.

"Shoot him! Shoot him now!"

I'm sure I do not need to tell you the person who yelled this was Commodore Spotswood.

In an instant, the air was thick with musket balls tearing into the ship's railing, mast, and rigging. The sudden volley swept over my head, forcing me to drop onto all fours. Crawling toward the front of the boat, I searched for a way to keep the soldiers from reaching the deck. The good news was the gangplank was as rickety and rotten as most of the rest of the *Dead Calm*. The bad news was it appeared to be sturdy enough to hold the soldiers charging towards me.

DEAD CALM, BONE DRY

With one swift, hard blow from the meat cleaver, I severed first one rope, then another, and shoved the gangplank away. Soldiers yelled; some fired muskets. The wobbly board ladder splashed into the water, as did the soldiers. Flat on my belly, I hacked through the thick ropes holding the vessel to the dock. All around me, musket balls thudded into wood.

"Hurry men! Seize that pirate before he escapes, again!"

Free of dock lines, the front of the *Dead Calm* slowly began drifting away from the dock. Taking a chance I wouldn't get shot, I sprinted back to the stern and the helm station.

"Ready ... Fire!"

A thunderous volley shattered the port railing and peppered the main mast. I reached the rear of the boat and found two soldiers climbing the stern line. I cut the rope clean with one blow, and the red-coated soldiers fell back into the water.

I was free of the dock and drifting away, but still an easy target. I sliced the topsail's halyard; the sail fell, fluttered momentarily, and filled. The *Dead Calm* shuddered and began gliding toward the harbor. Only then did I dare look back. The commodore stood at the edge of the dock, screaming for his men to shoot down the topsail, but it was too late. Only an expert sharpshooter could have hit the lines holding the sail aloft. I was free.

I grasped the ship's wheel and set a course for Rounder's Point, knowing full well I'd become the thing I'd been branded—a pirate.

CHAPTER TEN

Dog Gone It!

Within moments of escaping Commodore Spotswood and stealing the Dead Calm, I had cleared the harbor entrance and was sailing north toward Rounder's Point. Only took me a few minutes to spy Turtle Bill and Rebecca standing on a short beach in a protected cove. I dropped anchor and using Turtle Bill's small gig rowed ashore.

"I k-k-knew I could trust ye ter find me a ship!" Turtle Bill said, climbing into the gig. "Said ter yer missy, 'That lad's a stripling with spunk, he is. He'll find me a fine ship.' And so ye have. But say now, from the looks of her, she seems ter be riding low in tha water."

Turtle Bill had a point: the *Dead Calm* was listing, a nautical word that here means "falling over."

"Probably teredo worms," I said. "I'm pretty sure the hull is rotten with them."

Rebecca asked, "But is it seaworthy?" For our treasure hunt journey, she carried something like a soft duffle bag that, no doubt, was filled with girl stuff. She had ditched the long burgundy jacket with black lapels but still wore the paisley print vest, ruffled shirt, baggy black pants, and boots. She held her brown felt hat in her hand and let the breeze ruffle her hair.

"Was lucky to find this one unattended," I said, placing her bag near the stern of the gig. "But then when your fiancé started shooting at me, I had to move pretty fast."

"My fiancé? Just exactly w-w-who's ship did ye steal?"

"Never mind that," said Turtle Bill. "We have a vessel. That be all that matters. I do have one question, though. Who are those kids on deck?"

From the gig we all looked. Sure enough, a clot of boys and girls crowded along the rail. Some pointed at us, others waved. Amidst the children stood a tall, dark-skin woman with seashells dangling from the ends of her dreadlocks.

"No idea," I said. I did not think it a good time to mention that I'd found Snake's head boiling in a cauldron in the galley.

"Well, them youngins will have ter be shipped ashore. Or tossed over and swim."

Dirty faces stared back at me, eyes wide. I knew these children: or at least knew of them. They were the boys and girls I had seen herded into the corral after the prison ship docked in Port Charles. William Shakespeare had warned: "No room for riffraff and ruffians. Those boys, the healthy ones at least, will most likely be shipped off to work in the sugarcane fields. The diseased and deformed face a more gruesome fate." I guess what he'd meant was that they would be locked up on a leaky ship and left to starve.

"It looks they'll be sailing with us," I said.

"By thunder, this ain't a passage fer fair-weather sailors! Hearty souls and cool heads, them's the ones who sails with Turtle Bill."

"Keep your voice down," Rebecca said. "You want to hurt their feelings?"

"Feelings my foot. It's me who's giving orders, ain't it?"

"We cannot simply abandon those poor children on this beach."

"Rebecca's right. Especially if they are orphans, which I think they are."

"Besides, would it not be beneficial to have crew to help us raise and lower the sails?"

"It's me that's tha cap'n, not you two."

"Are we not a crew of pirates?" she said sharply. "And if so, should we not abide by the pirates' code?"

"Oh, and what be tha code ter which yer referring?"

At this point, we reached the back of the vessel, and the kids began clapping. Sort of made me feel important, though I knew I was not. The *Dead Calm* moaned and groaned as swells rolled under her. Turning blocks banged against spars. Without full sails, she sounded like a ghost ship.

"I believe the code Ricky is referring to is the code that says a crew can call a vote for a new captain any time they wish."

"But it's jest the three of us."

"And them," I said, pointing up at the kids still clapping for us.

"Tha two of you hatching a mutiny, are ya?"

Rebecca folded her arms, refusing to get out of the gig. "To save those children, yes."

"What I'd like to know, is how you propose to find the treasure once we reach Coffin Cay? Do you have a treasure map of some kind?"

"Aye, a map there is. Right in here." With his knuckle, he tapped the side of his head. "Find that gold and silver, I will, mark my word. But only as cap'n."

"And I will only agree to sail with you if you allow those children to sail with us," Rebecca shot back. "It would only take one word from me, and the commodore will send a fleet of ships after you. I am sure he would especially want to do so once he learns that Ricky stole his boat."

For a few seconds, the pair stared at one another. I shrugged and began climbing up the stern. It seemed like the smart move.

I'll be honest: I wasn't one hundred percent sure how things had deteriorated so fast. All I meant to do was row in and pick up two people and a dog. It certainly didn't bode well for a successful voyage. *Bode well*, by the way, is a phrase that in this instance meant, "probably ain't happening."

"F-f-fine. T-them misfits can come with us. Now for the love of Louie, Louie, kin we please get aboard hoist tha sails?"

"Wait! Where's my dog? We can't sail without him."

Turtle Bill glanced at Rebecca, who looked away as if avoiding the question.

"Where's Barnicle?"

"Wat yoa tink sneaking on dis boat?" I looked up. The dark-skin woman with dreadlock seashells leaned over the stern. She held a blowgun close to her lips. "Ax yoa a question!"

I had never been shot with a blowgun but could not imagine it would feel good.

"Uh, oh. Trouble mate," Turtle Bill said.

For a moment, I tore my gaze away from the scary-looking woman with the blowgun to see where Turtle Bill was looking. Jogging down the beach in formation were red-clad soldiers. Of course I do not need to tell you who was leading the charge of red-clad soldiers.

"But what about my dog?" I said, still trapped and hanging off the back of the *Dead Calm*.

"Ah'll explain once we be underway," said Turtle Bill. And with that, he whipped out his pistol and aimed it at the scary-woman with the blowgun.

For a few moments, the two faced off, neither showing any sign of backing down.

Then a musket ball shattered the stern's rear window. It was quickly followed by a second shot. Gun and blowguns were holstered, more lines let down, and within minutes the *Dead Calm* was once more sailing away under a hail of gunfire.

And still no one had explained where my dog was.

CHAPTER ELEVEN

THE SCARY-LOOKING WOMAN

"You lost Barnacle?"
"Couldn't be helped, mate. Mutt found a leg of lamb and ran off ter enjoy it all by his lonesome. No amount of calling did any good."

"He is telling the truth," said Rebecca. "We both tried, honest we did."

"Ah'm sure he'll eventually show up," Turtle Bill said. "Mutts of his stock always do."

"But we're sailing across the Caribbean Sea. How's a dog going to find us on the water?"

"There were a great many soldiers wandering about the waterfront," said Rebecca. "I suspect they were looking for you. Had we stayed and kept calling for the dog, I feel sure we would have been discovered."

Turtle Bill and Rebecca left. I suppose to get settled into their cabins. The children remained huddled on deck near the mast. I think they were scared. To be honest, I sort of was, too. Sailing a stolen vessel without any real crew was a huge ordeal in my book. I fixed my gaze on the horizon ahead of us and watched the ship's bow rise and fall. Behind me, the mountains of Rounder's Point faded from view. With nothing but a compass to guide me, I gripped the smooth wooden spoke of the ship's wheel and tried not to think of what would happen to Barnacle.

"What be yoa name?"

I whirled to find the scary-looking woman standing behind me. "Ricky. Ricky Bradshaw."

She grunted as if that was an unacceptable answer. "Wat yoa tink, I no hear yoa down dare earlier? Dat mon, he tink I no hear him, eater. But Hinny hear all." She eyed me in a way that made me wonder if she planned to kill and cook me, too.

"You ... killed Snake?"

"Wat you tink? I Bumbye pirate? Devil mon kilt him. Devil mon do bad tings to dat mon. Do utter tings, too."

I wasn't sure who the Devil mon was, but I had a hunch it was Commodore Spotswood. Or maybe Earl the Butcher.

"Dis be you's, ehy?" She fished my medallion out of her dress pocket: the one I gave Snake. Only now it was covered with blood.

"Is that why you killed Snake? So you could rob him?"

"I tol yoa! Devil mon kilt dat mon! I only keep fo de one who come fo it." She pressed the medallion into my hand.

"Yoa taka dis big boom boat 'n de gull faw away?"

"Gull?"

"Gull! Gull!" The scary-looking woman tossed her hair like girls in my school do when they're trying to get the athletic, good-looking, and popular boys to look at them.

"Oh, girl!"

"Gull, yes! Yoa take her faw, faw 'way from heah. Find dat treasure, eh?"

"Treasure? How do you know about that?"

"Hinny know all. See all, too. Yoa save gull, yes? Find dat island whit dat treasure. Find yoa fatta, too."

Father? How do you know about Dad?

"But fust yoa save dem dat no got no muddas and fattas. Hep dem little ones." She pointed at the kids huddled near the mast.

Which sort of confirmed what I'd suspected: the scary-looking woman was some kind of housemother for the orphans. She left and I returned to staring at the horizon, all the while checking the compass to make sure we were sailing due west. Due west was where I remembered seeing Coffin Cay on the chart the one time I'd plotted its longitude and latitude. Of course, finding a speck of island in such a large body of water was impossible, but I didn't dare tell anyone this. The longer they thought I knew what I was doing, the more time I had to come up with a plan.

At dusk, I lashed the helm and went below, found Turtle Bill in the first mate's cabin, and tried to wake him. "Your watch."

He stirred and slid his eye patch so he could look up at me.

"I'll be asleep in the captain's quarters," I said. "If you see anything ... land, sails, squalls, a giant squid, come get me."

Turtle Bill eased out of his bunk and gave me a two-finger salute. "Aye, aye, Cap'n. Keep a weather eye out and all."

He was mocking me. I didn't mind. I was exhausted and only wanted to sleep.

I knew part of his grogginess and sassy attitude came from all the drinking he'd done in The Blind Monkey. That was one reason I had stood the first two watches: I wanted to make sure we put some distance between us and Port Charles before turning the helm over to him. If we could sail for two days without running into trouble, I should spy Coffin Cay on the third day. Assuming we didn't stray too far to either side of the rum line.

DEAD CALM, BONE DRY

In the forecastle, I found Rebecca sorting piles of rope, canvas, block and tackle, extra wood for spars, caulking irons, bolts of cloth, clothes, and casks of pitch—everything necessary for making repairs to a leaky ship—which the *Dead Calm* obviously was. She'd scoured the vessel and placed all supplies in one area. Like a prudent sailor, she was taking inventory. I liked this girl. We made a good team. Or would have made a good team if she hadn't been constantly reminding me of how I left her on that island with our crew of Africans.

"So, how does it feel to be a pirate in command of a stolen prize?" said Rebecca.

"If I'm a pirate, it's your fault." I helped her lift a bolt of cloth and move it aside so she could inspect the contents of a steamer trunk. "I would never have agreed to steal this ship if not for you."

"You need not flatter yourself, Ricky Bradshaw. I am perfectly capable of taking care of myself."

"Didn't sound like it back at The Blind Monkey." I held up a frilly white shirt to see if it might fit me, but it looked too small, so I put it back on the pile. "Back there, it sounded like you needed my help getting away from someone."

"Whatever do you mean?"

"If you ask me, I think you're trying to escape Port Charles so you don't end up marrying the commodore." In the candle's light, I saw her cheeks become flushed.

"I can assure you my desire to sail aboard this horrid ship has nothing to do with the commodore's offer of marriage. It is the children I wish to save."

"Children? You didn't even know the kids were aboard until they rushed to the rail and began waving to us."

"Is that so? Was there another unguarded vessel you might have stolen? Any at all?"

I thought about it for like, two seconds, and realized she was right.

"While I was with my father at the fort, I heard things," she said. "Dreadful things. Turtle Bill seeks the treasure. He thinks having an abundance of gold and silver will make him rich. But I know true wealth is found in helping others. That is where our eternal treasures lie. And it is why I insisted on coming along on this despicable voyage. I am here to make sure these children have a chance at a better life than what they would have faced back in the sugarcane fields."

"Why not just tell your dad to treat the orphans better? He *is* the governor, after all."

"My father rarely ventures into the fields to witness the brutal conditions of his workers. He leaves the security of the island and its commerce to the commodore. And it is not my place to suggest to him how he should govern."

What she said made sense. I doubt Mom would appreciate me telling her how to run her routes or drive her truck. "So will you?"

"Will I what?"

"Marry the commodore?"

She folded another shirt and laid it on the pile. "I know men can change with the Almighty's help. I pray it will happen with the commodore."

"You didn't answer my question."

She stuffed a pair of pants into the trunk and said, "You should make your way to your cabin. Your watch will be here before you know it."

I did and fell asleep as soon as my head hit the flat pillow.

CHAPTER TWELVE

DEAD IN THE WATER

A sense of stillness awakened me. When sailing the lift and fall of the vessel becomes a part of your consciousness. Sail long enough and you hardly pay attention to the sounds of water rushing past the hull, howl of the wind, snapping of sails ... tilt of the vessel. The *Dead Calm* creaked as if abandoned.

I made my way on deck and found that we were dead in the water. Not a breath of air moved. Sails hung limp. Turning blocks clanked against wooden spars. Stars shone brightly against a black sky.

Rubbing sleep from my eyes, I said to Turtle Bill, "How does she sail?"

"When thar's wind, like a f- f-fat wench who's had too much rum."

"How long's it been like this?"

"Not more'n hour. Biting black flies showed up soon as tha wind stopped. Vicious little buggers they are. Night." Turtle Bill disappeared down a deck hatch.

I roamed the deck, checking on things. The children and scary-looking woman had done a fine job of transforming the *Dead* Calm into a ship-shape vessel. Sort of made me feel proud.

"Some captain you are." Rebecca joined me on deck, resting her elbows on the port rail. "You appear to have sailed us into a hole in the wind."

"Wasn't me." I wandered over to a water barrel. "Turtle Bill's doing." I dunked my head in warm seawater, rinsing my face.

"Excuses, excuses. Are you not the captain?" She leaned back on the rail and crossed her ankles. In the stars' faint light, her bare feet, white and smooth, stood out against the deck's dark planks. The top two buttons of her shirt were undone and her shirttail untucked. Rebecca's corn silk hair had the messed-up appearance of someone just waking up, which, oddly enough, only made me more attracted to her.

"You're right. It's my fault." Sarcasm is always the wrong response, but I was exhausted and needed a couple more hours of sleep. I shoved my head all the way under. The tepid salt water rinsed away the last traces of sleep from my eyes. I shook my head, slinging water the way a wet dog might. "You know why they call stretches of water like this the doldrums?"

"Am I going to care?"

"Because when ancient mariners sailed into calms like this, the crew would call to the quartermaster, 'Let de old rum flow.'"

"I hardly think that is where the term comes from."

"Kid you not. I read it in a book back home."

"Did you read anything about how to find wind? I am anxious for this trip to be over."

"Here," I said, taking her hand, "let me show you." I led her to the ship's stern railing and pointed at the horizon. I expected her to pull away, but she didn't. "Might get some wind from those clouds. Maybe some rain, too. Then again, it might miss us completely."

"You say that like you do not even care."

"Oh, I care. But there's nothing I can do about the wind." She released my hand and turned to face the front of the ship, bracing herself against the railing. "How close are we to Coffin Cay?"

Our faces were only a few inches apart.

"Let me show you."

I pulled Turtle Bill's cloth chart from my hip pocket and knelt on one knee, placing it flat on the deck. Lifting the lantern that served as the vessel's stern light, I placed it next to the chart. As Rebecca leaned close I detect the faint aroma of pine from where she'd been handling pitch in the storage room.

"This is Port Charles," I said, tapping the chart. "And this ..." I walked my fingers all the way off the chart until they're almost touching her knees, "is where I think Coffin Cay is."

She leaned closer, her breath warm on my cheek. "Where are we?"

I stabbed the chart close to its edge. "I'm guessing we're somewhere around here."

"How can you be certain Coffin Cay is out there? Turtle Bill said it was a ghost island that cannot be found except by those who already know its location."

"Turtle Bill's a fool. You can't hide an island. If this chart is even close to accurate, I'll find it."

I said this mostly to make her think I knew what I was doing. As I've already said, finding one small island in the middle of a large body of water is almost impossible.

I folded the chart and tucked it back into my hip pocket. "What's your real reason for going to Coffin Cay?"

"What do you mean?"

"Before, down in the storage room, you told me the main thing you cared about was getting the children safely away from Port Charles. Seems to me any port between here and Coffin Cay would do. I know it would be easier to find Cuba than it would Coffin Cay."

"The children are my first priority, but my father has certain ideas about how I am to act, whom I am to marry. How I am to conduct myself as the governor's daughter. I, on the other hand, have different ideas. My father says I am to prepare myself for the day when I will marry and raise a family. That is the way of women in England. But I shall not spend my life taking orders from a man. Not even my husband."

"Seems to me you were born about three hundred years too early."

"Whatever is that supposed to mean?"

"Just saying that you would have fit right in with the girls in my class. They're smart, independent, and good at running things."

"I cannot be sure, but I think you just paid me a compliment."

"Suppose, by some miracle, we do find the treasure," I said. "And suppose Turtle Bill divides the shares as agreed upon, which I doubt he'll do. What would you do with your portion?"

"Buy influence. You see, while Commodore Spotswood is not a blood relative of my father's family, he is my mother's nephew. Since Father has no male offspring, the governorship will no doubt pass to whomever I marry. But I have no intention of marrying the commodore. My plan is to accumulate enough influence and power to assume my father's position."

"You plan on becoming the governor? Seriously?"

"Why not? I can be . . ." she hesitated, casually stroking the side of my arm with her fingernails, "very persuasive. The commodore has the British Royal Navy at his disposal, not to mention the power of his courts, which you yourself have witnessed. My share of the treasure will secure me a place in parliament back home." She stood and looked across the dark sea. "Now tell me plainly. Can you locate this treasure island?"

"I think I can find it, sure. Even if it's not shown on this chart. When I saw the coordinates on Barnacle's belly, I memorized the numbers the same way I do when I'm trying to learn a new gym locker code. Based on our speed made good over water, I'd say we're less than one hundred miles away from Coffin Cay. No more than two days away."

This was absolutely the nicest conversation I'd ever had with Rebecca since before I smashed the *Black Avenger* on the reef and left her on the island with our crew of Africans. Which, of course, meant the moment would not last.

"But all that's assuming we have wind," I said, 'Which right now we do not. So that's a problem."

"They have wind."

"Who?"

"Them," Rebecca said, pointing.

At first I didn't see what she was pointing at. The sky was dark, sea dark. Then, as a sliver of moonlight stretched across the water, the silhouette of a ship appeared on the horizon.

"Can't be." I removed the spyglass from its holder and dialed in the focus. The vessel's topsail showed clear. Within seconds another sail appeared, then a third. The ship was large, certainly larger than the *Dead Calm*.

"Be," said Rebecca.

I'm sure I do not need to tell you that her snarky come back ended our nice conversation.

"Ah, mate? Might I 'ave a word with ya?"

I glanced over my shoulder. Turtle Bill was coming up from a deck hatch.

"Can it wait? I'm kinda busy, here."

"But it's deadly important."

"In a sec. I need to find out if that ship is friend or foe."

"Ship?" Turtle Bill took the spyglass from me. "She's coming on, and fast, she is."

"I can see that."

We could all see that: even without the spyglass. A little more of the moon peeked over the horizon. In its light, the vessel's sails were now clearly visible.

"Um, she'll be trouble fer sure," Turtle Bill said. With the black patch over his eye and the spyglass in his hand, he looked like a character from a Disney pirate movie. "You'll not outrun that ship, not without wind."

"I know that."

"Not with wind, either."

"But we should at least try, do you not agree?" Rebecca said.

Turtle Bill pivoted to face us. "We got bigger problems than that ship, missy."

I said, "What could possibly be worse than being captured by pirates or the British navy?"

"Worms. They've tunneled through the hull. We're sinking."

CHAPTER THIRTEEN

THE PHANTOM SHIP

Turtle Bill's words sent me racing to the ship's side. I peered over at and into the black water. Sure enough, the bearded band of sea grass that was the ship's boot strip was under water. We were sinking and fast.

"What now, Captain?"

"Yes, mate, what she said?"

We needed a plan and fast. I could hurry below and try to plug the holes in the hull, but how many holes were there and what would I stuff them with?

"How much pitch did you find in the forecastle?"

"Some. Not a lot."

So plugging the holes probably isn't an option.

"How may gigs do we have?"

"What the devil does that matter?" asked Turtle Bill.

"How many?"

"Bill's. Those you see on deck," said Rebecca. "That's it."

So some, I thought, *but not a lot.*

Once more, I aimed the spyglass at the horizon, only this time hoping to see a friendly flag: though to be honest, I wasn't sure what a friendly flag would look like, exactly. A half-moon peeked over the horizon. Its light painted a wide, golden ribbon on the dark sea, making it easy to see the silhouette of the ship against its pale face. Had we not been sinking in a stolen ship, the image would have, you know, been one of those postcard moments.

She was a large vessel, probably twice our length. I could not count the number of cannon barrels jutting out from her gunports, but there were certainly enough to blast us out of the water.

I was still watching the ship when a puff of smoke belched from its bow cannon. The blast had barely registered with me when a ball came screaming overhead and splashed harmlessly in the water.

"Warning shot," Turtle Bill said unnecessarily. "They'll mean business with tha next one."

"How is it they can find wind and you cannot?"

I scanned the deck, ignoring Rebecca's comment. "Do we have a white flag?"

"For what?" she said.

"Yer not thinking of surrender, are ye mate?"

Another cannonball came hurtling toward us. It smashed into our stern just below the aft castle and sent us diving for cover. At this point, I should mention that the kids sleeping on deck were awake and screaming and crying. So that wasn't helping matters.

On my belly I aimed the spyglass. It was a three-master with not one but two decks of gunports. She was close enough now that I could see the Union Jack flapping from her mast. If it was not the commodore's ship, then it had to be one in his fleet.

"Start building rafts."

Turtle Bill, also on his belly, looked at me as if I had zucchini growing out of my ears. "From what? Do ye have a carpenter shop aboard that I'm not aware of?"

"Find whatever tools you can and tear up the deck, if necessary. I think I saw some wood for extra spars below on the gun deck. Bring as much as you can on deck, and let's get to work."

"You are not thinking of abandoning ship, are you?" Rebecca asked.

"No."

Abandoning ship was absolutely what I was thinking.

"And make sure your gig is ready to launch," I said to Turtle Bill. "You know, in case we need to …"

"But if we abandon ship, how will we ever make it to Coffin Cay?" said Rebecca.

"Right now, I'm just trying to make it until tomorrow."

CHAPTER FOURTEEN

CASTAWAYS

I watched the *Dead Calm* gurgle out of sight. Not one of my proudest moments, but at least none of us were dead. Only the *Dead Calm* was dead. If there was some message in the fact that the air and sea were calm, I missed it. So far I'd skippered two boats: the *Black Avenger* and *Dead Calm*. Both sank. So I wasn't feeling all that great about my boat captaining skills.

Turtle Bill was in his gig with the scary-looking woman. I still did not know her name. I decided to start calling her Hinny. It figured Turtle Bill would be the first off the ship and take the best boat. Pirates always look out for themselves; that much I'd learned.

Rebecca and seven girls occupied the larger of the makeshift rafts we'd cobbled together. I crowded on among eight scared, smelly boys who mumbled and grumbled. Our raft was made from deck planks we ripped up and lashed together with that rope Rebecca found. On each there was a mount for a small mast, but I didn't dare try to raise the sail. I was waiting to see what sort of ship was bearing down on us.

"If it's British, we do intend to make ourselves known, do we not?" Rebecca's raft is so close I can almost reach out and touch her.

"Stop talking."

"Even if it is the commodore, we must surrender."

"I'm not looking to get hung a second time. I'll take my chances on this raft."

"But what of the children?"

"Tha lad has a point, missy." With Turtle Bill's gig close by, we'd formed something of a small triangle. "Even with my one bad eye, I kin tell she's a warship and a big one. Tha lad and me 'ill swing from a yardarm if we're picked up, of that ye kin be certain."

"Perhaps you are mistaken. Perhaps you merely thought you saw the Union Jack."

Rebecca was trying to sound hopeful. I made another scan with the spyglass and saw five staysails, all blowing full. With that much canvas, the phantom ship could beat against the wind, making her fast in all types of weather. There was no doubt she was British. The Union Jack flew from atop her mast.

"When she gets closer keep your head down and don't look up," I whispered. "Not even for a second."

The waiting was unbearable, but it beat swimming. I peeked to see if anything remained of the *Dead Calm*. Other than some loose planks floating about and a few bananas that had escaped the galley, the water was clear of debris. It was like the ocean had swallowed the vessel. The gentle slapping of water against Turtle Bill's gig let me know that our small fleet remained intact. From the girls' raft came whimpering and sniffling. A boy on our raft farted; the other boys laughed.

Gradually, the swooshing of water slicing past the ship's hull drowned out the girls' hiccupping sobs. Murmuring voices and flapping sails grew louder. I peeked. The great ship was less than fifty yards away, half a football field. Her deck was aglow with lanterns.

Here was the good news: clouds had moved in, cloaking the moon's light. But if the ship hung around long enough and the clouds moved, the crew on deck would see us for sure.

More lanterns appeared. I caught sight of figures leaning over the railing, staring down at the water. I dropped my head and stopped peeking. A bell clanged twice—not a good sign.

"Ricky?"

Without lifting my face I whispered, "What?"

"I am frightened."

"Stop talking."

I was pretty sure our small fleet was beyond the glow of deck lanterns, but I didn't dare check to make certain. Instead, I slowly tucked my chin in the crook of my elbow so that my arm hid my eyes and part of my face.

"Launch the rowboats, men!"

I'm sure I do not need to tell you who said that.

"If there are survivors out there, I want them brought aboard! Brought aboard and hung for piracy! Are my orders clear?"

If? They haven't seen us.

I lifted my eyes long enough to see longboats go over the ship's side.

We were dead: dead in the water. Just like the boat I'd stolen that sank.

CHAPTER FIFTEEN

Soul Survivors

The fleet of longboats fanned out across the water. Steady hands held lanterns over the bow, illuminating the faces of crewmembers. Every few moments, one or two boats would stop to lift a piece of wood from the water and toss it back: bits of broken spars, rigging ... all that was left of the *Dead Calm*.

I dipped my hand in the water and whispered to Rebecca, "Follow me."

"Follow where?"

"Just do as I say."

In my peripheral vision, I saw Turtle Bill catch wind of what I had in mind. He angled his gig to fall in behind the girls.

I didn't dare look back. Not for a while. But when I did there were so many lanterns behind us it looked like a strand of white Christmas tree lights strung out on the water. We'd put some distance between the longboats and us but not enough. I could tell from the way the lights moved across the water that the British sailors were finding less debris and coming towards us faster. Thank goodness flashlights hadn't been invented, yet. If they had, we'd have never stood a chance. Already, the two ends of the string of boats were in line with my raft. They were forming a net to catch us.

Fishermen do the same thing with a seine net. Toss it out, let the weighted bottom drop, and once it's properly stretched, those holding the ends slowly advance, making a U-shape bulb in the water. It would only take another minute or so before the outer longboats passed us and begin to draw the net tight, catching us.

"This way! Think I see something!"

The excited call came from ahead of me. I whirled and saw a dark figure sitting alone in a smaller boat directly in front. Somehow, the man in the smaller boat had managed to circle around without me noticing. Now, he was using the glow of lanterns from the other longboats to illuminate the silhouette of rafts and Turtle Bill's gig.

Smart.

And stupid on my part.

A thought came to me. Several, actually. Most of the thoughts had to do with what Earl the Butcher had warned that had to do with me finding my dad so I could kill him and me running into *marauding pirates, worms tha size of yer fingers, rats big as yer arm: squalls and shipwrecks and boiling hot days adrift at sea ... coral reefs sharper than a dirk and tombs filled with treasure and dead men's bones.* I wondered if me losing the *Dead Calm* was what he meant by shipwrecks. Here was another thought I had. Actually it was more like a memory.

Mom's dad used to watch a movie called *The Outlaw Josey Wales*. He watched in something called a VHS tape. If he could have been anything in the world, I think my granddad would have wanted to be a Confederate soldier during the Civil War.

He used to dress up and go to reenactments. I never saw him do this, but Mom said he went to see granddad in his Confederate camp a few times. My point is granddad and me used to watch *The Outlaw Josey Wales* a lot. Like every time I visited.

The thing I remember about the movie was the way Josey was a loner. He didn't like being around people. But he set off to find this man who had killed his wife and son and along the way he picked up people: another Confederate soldier, Cherokee chief, Navajo woman, and an old settler woman and her daughter. They were all depending on Josey to save them from something, but all Josey wanted to do was find the man who killed his wife and son.

That's sort of the way I felt. All I wanted to do was find out if the rumor about Dad was true and then get back home to Quiet Cove, but along the way I'd picked up a pirate, a governor's daughter, a dog that I lost, a scary-looking woman, and a bunch of orphans. It goes without saying that they expected me to protect and deliver them, so I won't say it. Except I will mention that I pretty much felt like I'd let everyone down.

Splat, splat, splat!

A few drops at first, then a hissing rush. Sheets of rain moved across the water so fast I lost sight of Rebecca's raft. Drops struck hard like silver marbles falling from the sky. The ring of lanterns grew dim. It was a monsoon-like rain, and it could not have come at a better time. From within the muffled roar of falling rain came the clanging of a bell: three times.

By the time I paddled back to Rebecca's raft, most of the longboats were at the warship, their lanterns ringing it. Though I could not clearly see the sailors at work through the rain, the flicker of lights rising let me know the longboats were being hoisted back aboard.

"Think they'll come back once the rain stops?" Rebecca asked too loudly.

DEAD CALM, BONE DRY

I shrugged, afraid to say anything out loud. She got her answer minutes later. The hard pounding of the rain lessened. It became easier to see the longboats against the ship's side. Still they continued to ride up as sailors pulled on ropes fed through block and tackle.

Another call went forth. Sails dropped. There came a sharp *POP,* and wind filled the topsail. Within minutes the warship's stern lantern became lost in rain and blackness.

I don't mind telling you: I was relieved to see the ship sail away. Cold. Wet. Exhausted. But relieved. Sure, we were alone and adrift on rafts and Turtle Bill's one gig, but at least I was not swinging by the neck.

Our goal now was to survive the night.

CHAPTER SIXTEEN

First Day as Castaways

You can smell land before you see it. This is especially true when you are adrift at sea on a raft. The sweet smell of damp soil and pine is the fragrance of hope. Hope and help. So I lay on my back, breathing in warm, moist air as the day's first light bled red across purple clouds. We'd survived our first night at sea as castaways.

Overhead, a gull circled, all the while squawking as if announcing there was food to be had. But there was no food. The scary-looking old woman was supposed to grab bananas and whatever she could find from the galley before the *Dead Calm* sank, but she forgot. I eyed the gull. It wasn't what you would call KFC quality, but if I could trap the bird and break its neck, maybe we'd have wings for breakfast.

Had I been back home, I would have been eating breakfast. But if I had been home, I also wouldn't have been on a raft in the middle of the Caribbean Sea with a bunch of smelly boys.

DEAD CALM, BONE DRY

The way the gull circled our tiny fleet made me wonder if there were fish nearby. *Fish would be good,* I thought. *I could go for some sushi right about now.*

I made a quick check of our raft, looking for anything that might serve as a rod and line. There was the raft's rudder, but it was too big. The rudder was one of the pieces of wood I found in the storage room of the *Dead Calm's* forecastle. Same with the small mast and boom and sail we'd snagged before she sank. The girls' raft and Turtle Bill's skiff were rigged pretty much the same way. We were not what you would call the Niña, the Pinta, and the Santa Maria, but we were sailing toward land. At least, I hoped we were sailing toward land. Without a knot meter, sextant, or GPS, it was impossible to say for sure.

But I smelled land, and that was a good sign.

CHAPTER SEVENTEEN

DAY TWO ADRIFT AT SEA

Festering sores covered my body from where saltwater spray and the unrelenting sun beat upon me. I could have really used a big tube of Neosporin and Band-Aids, but things like Neosporin and Band-Aids hadn't been invented yet. I lay on my back on the raft, my right arm thrown over my eyes to knock down the glare of the sun. I decided if I ever did make it back home to Quiet Cove I would never ever simply lay out by a pool or on a beach again. I'd had all the sun I ever wanted.

I would have to make a decision soon. I could keep sailing west and hope to run into Coffin Cay, or turn north and try to find some other, larger island. Cuba, maybe.

I sat with my back against the small mast and looked over at Rebecca's raft. She was asleep, her body wedged between seven girls. That was all my crew did: sleep, rest, complain that they were hot, thirsty, and hungry.

DEAD CALM, BONE DRY

I wasn't ready to panic, but if we didn't make landfall soon, somebody was going to die. And that somebody was probably going to be me.

CHAPTER EIGHTEEN

THE FLYING DUTCHMAN

For days we'd drifted westward using small scraps of canvas rigged to a single, short mast to push us along. The sails helped, but not enough. We were lost, famished, and without fresh water I was pretty sure some in our crew would be dead by morning. I hate to sound so morbid, like all hope was lost, but there is no point in lying: we were desperate, and I didn't have a good plan, bad plan, or any plan. I was out of ideas.

Rain began to fall at dusk on the fifth day. We all turned our heads skyward when the skies opened, parted our lips, and drank in the warm, fresh water. Lying on our backs we soaked in the rain's wet relief. Salt water washed off sunburn; tattered clothes got a good rinsing. During the first few minutes of the deluge the air remained mostly still with only a hint of breeze. But gradually the rain became heavier, pounding us like it had the night we'd escaped the British warship. What began as blessed relief turned into a torrential downpour that left us chilled to the bone.

Without any way of escaping the rain we huddled together and tried to stay warm. Seems odd, I know, to be complaining at the heat one moment and say we're freezing the next, but the fact is, the body's temperature is 97.7 degrees. Water temperature in all oceans is several degrees below that. The Indian Ocean is the warmest, but it's only around 82 degrees. That means if you are in the water you'll eventually die of hypothermia. My point is this: it doesn't take much to make you cold on a boat or raft.

The breeze that followed the rain came from the northeast and steadily built into a howling gale that threatened to tear apart the rafts. Water sloshed up between planks; ropes stretched and broke. Boys on my raft held onto each other to keep our small vessel from being torn apart.

One look Rebecca's way confirmed my fears: theirs had split in two. Two girls lay on their bellies, legs dangling in water while they clung to the remainder of their portion of the raft. She called to me for help, but there was nothing I could do. We'd drifted too far away, and I'd completely lost sight of Turtle Bill's gig.

In the midst of all this, a cloud of heaviness settled over me. Not fear. This was a kind of hopelessness I'd never experienced. Not even when I'd had my seizure and fallen into the creek had I felt anything like this. Or when I'd stood on the gallows with a noose over my head. The terror I felt reached all the way to my soul. I realized for the first time in a very real way that the hopelessness would never leave. That even if I died right then on the raft the loneliness, isolation, and desperation would be with me for eternity. Soon it became clear why. Amidst the terrible storm, a strange, phosphorescent green ghostly glow approached. *A ship of some kind*, I thought. For a moment I almost called out. Then the vessel's bow pierced the sheets of rain, and I knew in an instant it was the *Flying Dutchman*.

Instantly the wind stopped, but not the rain. The air became dead calm.

It's true! The ghost ship exists! I checked to see the reaction of the others; no one seemed to notice the vessel. Probably because they all remained on their backs with eyes closed.

There's a term sailors use when sailing short-handed. They call it sailing with a skeleton crew. Before me was just such a sight—only the crew that lined the deck was nothing but skeletons. Though I could clearly see each man's features I could also see *through* him to the point where tendons and ligaments hung on bones and joints. M*en* crowded along the rails. Some opened mouths wide, skulls bobbing as they laughed and pointed bony fingers at me. I stared in astonishment at the sight of the phantom sailing ship with its black masts and blood-red sails.

I knew from reading pirate books that the *Flying Dutchman* was captained by De Vliegende Hollander. Because it was a *ghost ship*, the *Dutchman* could never make port. The ship and its crew were doomed to sail the oceans forever. If hailed by another ship, the crew of the *Flying Dutchman* would try to send messages to land, or to people long dead. And simply seeing the phantom ship was a warning that something bad was about to happen—like being adrift on a raft without any food or water and then seeing a ship crewed by dead men wasn't bad enough.

I elbowed the boy next to me. He opened his eyes, looked up, and around. I jerked my chin upwards, trying to warn him that we were about to crash into a ghost ship, but he didn't seem to notice or care. The hull of the *Flying Dutchman* bumped against one corner of our raft, causing us to slowly turn. And still not a soul around me stirred. It was like everyone was in a trance and blind to the danger.

Gradually I became aware that the air had grown considerably warmer. Not muggy or humid like is normal in the tropics, but an intense dry heat. Furness heat. Campfire heat. Cupping my hand over my eyes, I squinted against the drizzling rain and saw nothing except the massive, curved hull towering above us. The stench of soggy, stinking seaweed and what smelled like rotting corpses made me want to barf.

"Hey, Cargo!" Above me one of the crew leaned over the railing. Only the man didn't have a head. Well, he did have a head, but he had tucked it under his arm like a basketball. "Heads up!"

The skeleton-like ghost snatched his head from under his arm and threw it at me. It splashed the water, bobbed and turned. A man's gaunt face came into view.

"Get it?" Snake's decapitated head said to me. "Heads up?"

"No talking to the cargo!" I'm sure I do not need to tell you who said that.

"You hurt me bad, mate."

"I said no talking to the cargo! We are not here to play to dream or to drift. We have bills to pay and loads to lift. One of you fellers let a rope down so we can pull that corpse aboard."

"See you on board," Snake's head said and sank from view.

So that was a problem—dead men throwing heads at me and Earl the Butcher threatening to bring me aboard a ghost ship.

A rope dropped over the ship's side. Only it wasn't a normal rope. It was a rope with a noose on the end. And the noose was behaving like the flared head of a cobra about to strike. The flared noose expanded, lifted, and waggled over my head before gently settling on my hair.

So that was also a problem—a rope that acted like a deadly serpent and its noose that was, at that very moment, slithering over my ears and dropping onto my nose.

Right then, faint as a whisper … barely audible over the *splat, splat* of rain striking water, another voice called to me. "Come back, Ricky."

I looked up and around, down and into the water. No bobbing head, no skeleton-ghost.

"Your mom and I, we miss you."

The slithering noose slipped over my nose and cheeks and bumped my chin.

"Let it go, Ricky. Forgive me and let it go."

Dad?

The noose synched tight; I grabbed at my throat and …

The noose vanished; the ship vanished. Dad's voice trailed off. As it did I heard him say, "See you soon."

CHAPTER NINETEEN

Lost

A distant roaring noise startled me. I rolled over and stared at the limp sail and gray-pink sky. After the appearance of the *Flying Dutchman* I had tried to make sense of the aberration. In doing so, I'd drifted off to sleep. Judging from the sky's rosy hue, daybreak couldn't be far off. I pushed myself up and searched for the source of the low, whooshing sound that had awakened me.

Ahead lay an island. Palm trees grew thick, right down to the water's edge. Behind them, tall pines spread inland to the base of a conical-shaped mountain whose peak was shrouded in clouds. Towering above the beach and cove was a steep rock cliff with two large caves that gave the rock face the look of a skull.

I nudged my crew awake.

For days, the boys had laid sprawled about like zombies. Now, they sat up and stared at the island with looks of disbelief. The girls on Rebecca's raft tried to join in the celebration, but most were too tired to lift their heads. I swam over to Turtle Bill's gig and shook his shoulder. He rose on elbows, peered over the side, and gave me a faint nod of acknowledgment. No reaction at all from Hinny. She was tucked into a fetal position in the bow of the gig.

    Back on our raft, I focused my attention on the long line of breaking surf that stood between the beach and us. I was sure there had to be a cut through the reef. There usually is around islands. Coral thrives in warm salt water, and when cool, fresh water runs down hills and into coves, it stunts the coral's growth. That's where the inlets form. But I didn't see any such channel. The surf appeared to be one long barrier that kept us from reaching the safety of the beach beyond. No matter, I thought. I've been on this raft too long. We're going in. Dead or alive, I'm burying my face in sand.

    On my order, the boys and girls and Turtle Bill manned their oars, adjusted sails, and aimed for the island.

    Booming surf warned of the danger ahead. There is a pattern to sets of waves. A lot of the time a group of four waves will arrive within seconds of each other. The longer the space between waves, the farther the storm that's producing the swells. I waited for the last wave of a set to roll under us, watched as its crest feathered back, and ducked as spray blew over and onto us from the breeze blowing down the island's hills. When it exploded on the reef, I looked back to check on the rest of our small fleet. The water ahead was relatively flat, now. No more breaking waves. But they would be coming, soon. I could already see humps on the horizon.

    I nodded to the two boys manning our oars; they paddled with a devilish fury. We were committed now, surging ahead. Coral heads could clearly be seen mere feet below. If a wave broke on us, now, its force would impale us on razor sharp-coral spikes. There was no need to tell the boys to paddle harder. Everyone saw the danger we faced.

I manned the rudder, guiding us across the wide swath of calm water. For a few hopeful moments, I thought we might actually make it all the way in before the next set arrived. Then from behind, a shadow fell over us and I knew we were still too far out.

The wave rose from the deep like some monstrous leviathan.

It was hard not to marvel at the breaker's beauty, admire its smooth, translucent wall. The raft pitched sharply, and we plunged straight down as if falling off a skyscraper. I leaned back to keep the raft's leading edge from digging in. As the massive wall of green water threatened to pick us up and thrash us onto the reef, I pushed the tiller, guiding us down its face. We were in the *pipe*, getting *barreled. On a raft*, I thought. *How cool is this?* A blast of hissing spray soaked us, blinding me so I could not see ahead.

Then it was over. The wave was spent. Our small raft bobbed on calm water and slowed. Ahead lay a smooth white-sand beach dotted with flowering shrubs, tall and full of white blooms framed against dark green leaves.

From the front of our raft, one of the boys pointed back over my shoulder. I checked behind.

The surf zone was littered with debris from the girls' raft. Broken planks, a snapped mast. Small dark heads bobbed amid white foam. Hands waved for help. For a brief moment, I saw Rebecca swimming frantically, trying to get away from the next wave … except she was already being sucked up the face of its wall. In an instant, she became lost in the wave's collapsing barrel: hurled and tossed directly onto the reef.

Without waiting for her to surface, I swam towards where I'd last seen her.

CHAPTER TWENTY

Coffin Cay

Searching the water, I scanned the next set of approaching waves. No sign of Rebecca. I was, however, able to reach the girls. They'd formed a group amid the debris from the destroyed raft. After I made sure we still had seven girls, we swam in. I fell back onto warm, wet sand. I wanted to cry or scream, but I was so tired that all I could do was close my eyes and sigh heavily. The sun's rays dried my skin; the constant pounding of waves was hypnotic. Picturing Rebecca's face in the moon's glow the night we'd stood at the stern of the *Dead Calm* I wanted to cry.

You may be wondering why I didn't swim back out into the surf zone and keep looking for Rebecca. I thought about it. Wanted to. But I thought: *What's the point? No one could have survived that. It's a shallow reef and the waves are huge. If only I'd kept sailing down the coast and tried to find an easier place to come in. But I was in a hurry. I was ready to be done with this stupid voyage. And now, she's dead.*

I sat up, looked down the beach. Some of the kids had gathered around Turtle Bill and his gig. He knelt in sand, cradling the old woman in his arms.

Up until that point, I hadn't been sure Turtle Bill was even capable of caring about anyone but himself. But seeing him holding her like that and sobbing, I decided even murderous pirates have hearts. I hurried towards him to see if I could help, but I was too late. That much was obvious. The old woman was dead, her skin a ghoulish gray. Going almost a week without enough fresh water and nothing to eat had been too much for her. I put my hand on his shoulder but said nothing. It seemed like the smart move.

Some of the girls hugged him. Others covered their faces while they cried. Even the boys took it hard. I understood. Though they'd been locked in a forward room with no way to escape, she'd kept them fed and housed on the *Dead Calm*. In one of her gibberish moments of clarity, I'd managed to gather that the commodore had the keys to the room and that he was paying her to keep them alive until he could sell them to a planter on the island in need of cheap labor. If not for the old woman, they would still be prisoners of Commodore Spotswood.

Her loss hit me hard.

Which, of course, made me think of Rebecca.

I promised myself I would swim back out and keep looking. Her body deserved to be found and buried, not left bloated and washed up on some beach where birds and other animals would feed on her. That thought sickened me.

"Is she dead?"

I whirled. Rebecca stood behind me, soaking wet, sand splattered on her sun-brown face, arms, and feet.

"You're ... alive."

"No thanks to you. So what do we do now?"

"We give her a proper burial."

CHAPTER TWENTY-ONE

Funeral for a Friend

The old woman's funeral was a simple affair. Turtle Bill insisted on using his gig as a funeral pyre. I thought it was a bad idea and said so. We might need a sound skiff to explore the coast later, or—and this was a big one—escape the island if there was another tribe of head-hunting, man-eating savages. I suggested we use the boys' raft for the old woman's burial float. Turtle Bill would have none of it. He'd taken the old woman's loss hard; I didn't press the issue.

We laid the old woman in the gig and covered her with dead palm branches. The boys added dry coconut husks ... anything that would burn. The girls tossed on flower petals. It was all very touching: a scene I might have appreciated more if not for the heavy guilt I felt for stealing the *Dead Calm* with her and the kids aboard. No two ways about it, her death was my fault.

When everything was ready, Turtle Bill ignited the kindling with his fire striker and dropped it into the palm branches. The three of us—Turtle Bill, Rebecca and I—shoved the gig toward the breakers. An outgoing current helped take it past the shore break and toward the reef. There was very little chance it would make it past the surf zone, but this was how Turtle Bill wanted things done. I didn't argue.

The gig reached the breakers just as the last wave of a set died. The current (a rip current, really) continued to pull the gig seaward. It was moving so fast that by the time the next set approached, the funeral pyre was clear of the reef and drifting out to sea. I wouldn't call it a miracle, but it certainly was odd. And a testimony to the power of rip currents. If you're reading this and thinking you can swim out of a rip current, don't try. Michael Phelps couldn't outswim a rip. Relax and swim parallel to the shore. On your back, if you can, so you can see the sky and clouds and not panic. Treat your escape from the rip like a long, leisurely float on the water. Then when you're sure you're out of the current, angle towards the beach, still floating on your back.

[This water safety tip is brought to you by the good people at Pickle Pete's Pub, where you'll find all your favorite beverages and foods. *Pickle Pete's ... If it's not Pete's, it's not worth repeating.*]

Turtle Bill sniffed, wiped his nose with his shirtsleeve, and turned to me. "I got ter admit, mate, I had m-my doubts about ye being able ter find this island." There was a forced cheerfulness to his voice. "I dare say Thaddeus LaFoote himself couldn' 'ave laid a course any better'n you did. I seen you was the right sort fer this voyage the first time I laid eyes on ye. Showed your colors true, you may lay to that. Now then, thar's plenty of daylight left. What say ye and me hurry off ter find that cave 'fore dark."

"Sure we're on the right island?"

"'Course I'm sure. Wouldn't be offering ter go hunt fer the cave if I weren't."

"What about me?" Rebecca said.

Even though we had not discussed it, I was pretty sure I knew what Turtle Bill was thinking. And the thing I was thinking that he was thinking was this: *Without me soul mate around, someone has ter take care of the children.*

Which was pretty much exactly what he said. "Ye stay here and keep an eye on things."

"I will do no such thing! You will not leave me behind while you and Ricky go hunting for some great treasure."

"By thunder, we can't take all these children into the jungle."

"They're exhausted," I said, trying to help Bill out. "I'm exhausted. But Turtle Bill and I can move faster if it's just the two of us. They need food and water and rest."

"You mean me, that is what you are saying. That I need food and water and rest. So if that is what you are saying, say it."

"I promise, if Turtle Bill and I find the treasure, you'll get your share. Isn't that right, Turtle Bill?"

"Aye, ye 'ave ma word on it."

"The word of a lying pirate hardly carries any weight with me."

"If things are like Turtle Bill says, I'll be back before you have time to miss me." I quickly kissed Rebecca on the top of the head. "I promise."

"I sincerely doubt that."

CHAPTER TWENTY-TWO

A Surprise atop The Skull

I stood next to Turtle Bill, looking up at a towering rock face pitted with shallow indentions and deeper grottos. Two large caves proved the most interesting. They formed what looked like two eyes, beneath which were two oval-shaped cavities that could have passed for The Skull's nose. A protruding ledge marked the entrance to a gaping mouth. Atop the summit a wind-twisted tree bowed outward, its spindly limbs protruding over the edge.

Turtle Bill removed his tricorn hat and wiped his forehead with the back of his coat sleeve. For some time, he remained quiet, as if considering what to do next. I studied the large black vulture perched on the edge of one of The Skull's eye sockets and wondered what exactly we would do if we found a treasure. We did not have a ship. We did not even have a gig. We did not have a plan of any kind that would get us off the island *if* we found a treasure. In fact, if I'm being honest, the thing we should have been doing was working hard to make shelters and find food and fresh water because, you know, we were pretty much like the Swiss Family Robinsons, only without the organ in the tree house.

Looking up at the rock face, Turtle Bill said almost reverently, "El Cráneo." I didn't know what to say to that so I said nothing. "Tha first mate warned tha place be cursed—that them who stepped ashore would ne'er leave. Bet that bird is guarding dead men's bones."

"What bird?"

"The one what told me the story of this place."

"But I thought you knew of Coffin Cay because of the dog."

"I did. But then when I was in some pub, can't remember which one, now, I heard the whole tale."

"What tale?" Rebecca said.

"What are you doing here?"

"Same as you. Claiming my share of the treasure. What tale?"

"The island is cursed."

"You cannot put a curse on a whole island," said Rebecca as if she were a professor of religion at Duke University. "Or even a person."

"Cursed it is and then some," said Turtle Bill.

"Rebecca's right. Things like curses don't really exist."

"That so. LaFoote swore he a curse on you, didn' he? Said ye would die a pirate's death? Sentenced to swing as a pirate, ye were and here ye are a pirate hunting treasure on a ghost island. If yours be not a cursed soul, I'm tha queen's footman."

"You need to go back and stay with the kids," I said.

"What about the tale?"

"Some years back," Bill said, "a nefarious pirate named Calico Jack skippered a vessel named the *William*. The *William* was several days out of Nassau sailing east of the Bahamas when Calico Jack happened upon a sixty-gun Spanish galleon stuffed to tha gunnels with gold and silver and jewels. *Nuestra Señora de Riqueza*, she was. Returning from tha Spanish Main. *William's* crew captured the prize in a bloody fight and killed all its crew. Then Calico Jack put some of his crew aboard and continued east, flying under the Spanish flag while seizing tha rest of tha fleet. By the time tha three galleons and the *William* took shelter off a small island west of Hispaniola, the *William* was loaded down and wallowing in the water like fat sows."

"Hang on, how do you know all this?"

"Told ye 'twas a little bird that told me. See, thar's a settlement upriver of Spanish Town in Jamaica not far from where Calico Jack and his crew met their end. Talks freely, that parrot does. Or did after I lubricated its tongue with rum."

"You got a parrot drunk?" Rebecca asked.

"Birds gots vices same as men. Some fowls like worms and such. This one happened ter have a preference fer 'Kill Devil.'"

"He means rum," I said to Rebecca.

"I *know* what 'Kill Devil' is. My father calls it a hot, hellish, terrible liquor."

"Anyhow, Calico Jack got ter worrying 'bout being raided by pirates himself, so he made for Isla de Ataúd."

"Coffin Island," Rebecca said softly.

"Aye, 'tis called by them that knows those waters. Got a skull's face on its south facing beach. Souls of the dead roam its beaches. Can't be found except by them that's got the coordinates."

"Or by those making up this story," I said dryly.

"You two want ter hear the tale or don' ye?"

"Should we not be trying to find our way up to those caves?" Rebecca asked.

"She's right," I said. "Let's see if there is a path or steps or something."

Off we trekked into the jungle following a small creek. Right away, heavy, boggy ground and matted vegetation slowed our progress. Continuing inland the woods gradually changed from palms and banana trees to pines. Little by little the base of a low ridge began to come into view.

"Slowly and carefully the *William* eased into tha tiny harbor. Rest of tha day, all tha gold, silver, and jewels was ferried ashore in chests. Each man took his share according ter the agreement and went off ter bury it. 'Course not all of 'em came back, seeing as how they was pirates and pirates is known ter cut another man's throat over gold and silver."

We made our way into a thicket choked with briars and some plants with razor-sharp fronds. Barefoot and still wearing my ragged jeans, now cut-off shorts, from home, the fronds sliced my legs.

"At dusk, rum and brandy were broken out. Didn't take long before tha whole crew was shouting and shooting and splashing in tha water. Not Calico Jack though. He and his first mate, Trembles, kept sober. When all the crew was passed out an' in no condition ter notice, Jack and Trembles took thar three chest, two for tha cap'n, one for tha first mate, and went ashore to hide thars."

"I cannot imagine you learned all this from one man."

"Bird," Turtle Bill added. "Not a man. Fowl kept squawking about this treasure stowed away on a ghost island. I inquired of my waitress as to if I might speak to tha bird's owner. She directed me ter a back room where I found this British sailor. Or was 'fore he was caught sneaking into the governor's wife's bed. Was with a group of sailors the day they captured Calico Jack. Heard the account firsthand. Apparently that sailor repeated so often that the bird learned ter tell it better than the Brit."

The jungle air was stifling hot. Blue sky peeked through the thick treetop canopy.

"But what about the treasure?" I said.

"Once they reached tha beach, the pair came upon a goat path that led them to tha summit, Calico Jack tied a rope fast to a storm-twisted tree that grew over the edge and, using a block and pulley, tossed tha rope down. Together, the two men lowered tha first chest down until it settled on a ledge jutting out from a cave. Down they climbed and pulled tha chest inside. Twice more they done this. Was almost dawn 'fore they got those chest stowed away. By tha time Calico Jack and Trembles was back aboard tha *William*, tha crew was stirring. Pair made like they'd been aboard all night. Jones ordered the crew to weigh anchor, and the *William* sailed away."

Right then I spied a path angling around the base of the cliff. Bill stopped talking and looked at us expectantly.

"And?" said Rebecca.

"And what?" he said. "That's tha tale."

The path curved upward, leading around the back of the skull cliff.

Rebecca looked at the goat path, up at the steep cliff, and slapped another mosquito. "I'm going back. If you find treasure, you'll let me know."

"I will, but he may not," I said.

"Oh, I will know. If you don't come back, you found treasure. If you do come back and say you did not, I will know that you did. Either way, I know where this so-called treasure is, now."

I'll be honest: I wasn't following her logic one hundred percent but I didn't argue.

And about a half hour later, Turtle Bill and I reached the summit. Before us, the cobalt sea stretched south, east, and west as far as the eye could see. Behind us, looking north, lay scalloped valleys carpeted with lush green trees. A small waterfall soaked a deep ravine in a misty shower, turning the canopy a dark green. The scene was stunning. I would have appreciated it more if I had not been so scared of falling over the edge.

There was absolutely nothing to keep me from sliding down the smooth, curved dome of rock and falling to my death. Turtle Bill tossed me a small canvas sack. Inside were rope, block, and tackle brought from the *Dead Calm* for just this purpose.

"Tie that rope good and tight 'round that trunk. I'll winch ye down to that ledge."

"How about if I winch you down?"

"Can't. I'm dreadful feared of heights."

"And I'm afraid of dying," I said.

"Hurry, mate. Crawl on out to that tree. We ain't got all blessed day."

With the rope looped around my neck I crawled on hands and knees toward the scraggly tree. To my right and west lay a wide blue bay. Below on the beach, Rebecca walked towards the children. Some had gathered coconuts into a pile. I suppose to make a campfire. Others had stretched the two sails between trees. But what really had my attention—and not in a good way—was the large object farther down the coast.

"Hand me the spyglass," I said.

"What fer?"

"Just give it to me. I think I saw something."

"What sort of something?"

"Down the coast where that big bay is. A sail."

Turtle Bill crawled out a few feet so he could see around the curve of the summit, then still on his knees, put the scope to his one good eye. "Don't see nothing."

"Beyond that ridge, just past the tip of that headland."

Mumbling under his breath about how a good wind would blow him off the summit, he dialed in the focus. "Sink me!"

"What?"

"British warship. Tha commodore's ship, hast ter be. He must've followed us here. See fer yerself." Turtle Bill handed me the glass and lowered himself onto his stomach.

I swept the coastline until I caught sight of the Union Jack flying atop a mast. "But I never saw a ship, not once."

"Little matter that makes. Could be that was his plan all along. Make like he gave up looking fer us so that we'd lead him to Coffin Cay. Which ye did."

I'm sure I do not need to tell you that Turtle Bill's tone suggested the sight of a British warship anchored less than a mile from where the kids were making camp was all my fault.

I passed him the spyglass and backed away from the edge.

"Hold on, mate. Where do ye think yer going?"

"To warn Rebecca."

"The devil, ye say. That beach, it'll be swarming with redcoats in no time."

"Well, I have to do something!"

Turtle Bill took hold of my arm, stopping me. "Ye *are* doing something. Yer hunting treasure."

"I mean about Rebecca and the kids."

"What be yer plan when ye get down there? Fight a whole company of British soldiers all by yer lonesome?"

"If I have to, yes."

"Yer not thinking things through, mate. Tha commodore might fancy yer missy as his future bride, but I'll wager he loves gold and silver more'n that pretty face of hers. Find that treasure an' ye got some leverage. Try'n help yer missy right now and ye'll swing fer yer trouble."

Of course he was right. If we found treasure and could hide it someplace else, maybe I could negotiate swapping the treasure for the safety of Rebecca and the kids. But then I realized that was a dumb idea. The commodore would simply torture the kids or Rebecca or me until I told him where the treasure was.

"You'll have to get that treasure by yourself," I said, crawling back toward where the goat path ended. "I'm going to warn Rebecca."

DEAD CALM, BONE DRY

I'd only gone a short ways when Turtle Bill crawled up from behind me. "Mate, yer no good to me dead, but I'll cut ye gill-to-gill 'fore I'll let ye tell them soldiers 'bout the treasure down in that cave." He laid the blade of his dirk against my throat. "We clear?"

I nodded. It seemed like the smart move.

CHAPTER TWENTY-THREE

Caved In

"Ye might need this when ye get in that cave." Turtle Bill handed me a torch he'd cobbled together from dead vines, sticks, and dried leaves.

I tucked it into the waistband of my shorts. It was a straight drop all the way down to where small waves beat against the rocks at the base of the cliff. The view did not leave me with a good feeling about surviving our treasure hunt. I wanted to yell to Rebecca about the ship, but she and the kids were no longer on the beach. My hope was that she'd sensed something was up or heard the ship's sail snapping, and taken cover in the jungle.

I checked the rope. It was double-knotted and tight around the trunk. I'd made sure. Not that it mattered all that much. If the tree snapped, my knot-tying skills wouldn't count for much, and from the looks of the spindly trunk, that was a distinct possibility.

"You can do this, mate." Turtle Bill gave me a broad smile. "I have faith in ye."

I knew he was only saying that because he wanted the treasure, but it was nice to hear. I needed all the encouragement I could get. Scooting forward and taking a deep breath, I slid over the side. The tree groaned; I moaned "uh, oh" and gripped the rope tighter. Moving my hand down even an inch took all the courage I had.

"That ship be rounding the headland," Turtle Bill said. "Any second now, she'll start making her way up to where them kids be."

Like saying it that way was going to make me go faster. I'd already given up all hope of saving Rebecca and the kids.

I placed one hand below the other and eased down slowly. My heart was beating so hard it hurt. *This is crazy. What am I thinking? I can't hold onto this rope and climb down to a narrow ledge at the entrance to a cave. I'm such an idiot.* I kept banging my knees and elbows, and each time I did, another shower of pebbles fell onto the rocks below. When I'd dropped about twenty feet down, I passed between The Skull's two eye sockets. Same stupid vulture I'd seen from the beach sat on the edge, watching me. *Maybe he's hoping I'll become his dinner.* Another few feet, and I was in front of the opening that passed for The Skull's nasal cavity. It was more of a notch in the rock than an actual cave, but my sudden appearance startled a flock of nesting gulls. They went squawking and flapping past me so fast I almost accidentally let go.

"There yet?"

I didn't dare look up. Or down: just kept staring at my knuckles as I moved one hand over and beneath the other. Sweat poured off my forehead and trickled into my eyes. My arms ached; palms burned. Finally, my foot found the ledge jutting out from The Skull's mouth.

The shelf was about two feet wide and twice that long. I had no idea if it would support my weight, so I hung onto the rope, lowering myself into a crouch. "Made it!" I shouted up to Turtle Bill.

"Any treasure?"

"I'll let you know after I get inside!"

I fell back into The Skull's mouth and released the rope. I could still reach it if need be, but should the wind start howling, retrieving my safety line would become interesting. I made a final scan of the beach. Still no sign of Rebecca or the kids.

When my eyes adjusted to the cave's dimness, I scanned my surroundings. Except for a few feathers and some bird droppings, the grotto was empty. The cave was bigger than I expected. Certainly big enough for me to stand. Using Turtle Bill's fire striker, I ignited his homemade torch. Leaves popped and hissed. The torch didn't provide much light, but it was all I had, and if I didn't hurry, I wouldn't even have that.

Holding it at arm's length, I continued creeping towards the back of the cave, eased around a curved wall and proceeded down a short incline. The torch was all but spent by the time I reached the back of the cave. There remained just enough light coming from the cave's mouth for me to make out a pit in front of me. Had I been walking in the dark, I would have probably fallen into the pit. Resting against one side was a crudely constructed wooden ladder with rungs made from short limbs. Several of the rungs had rotted through. I carefully placed my foot on the first rung. It held. Then I did the same with my other foot.

There was no way to hold the torch and climb down; I dropped it. The good news is the pit wasn't that deep. Bad news is, when the torch hit it all but went out. Only a few embers remained glowing orange.

If you're expecting to read that the rung snapped and I fell, then you pretty much have a good idea of what I was thinking. Basically, I clung to the ladder's two supports and hoped the whole thing didn't collapse.

Climbing down was like descending into an empty well. Some of the ladder's rungs were missing; others were too unsteady to support my weight. When I finally reached the bottom, the air was surprisingly cool. But it wasn't the air temperature that chilled me: it was the bones and skulls.

Other treasure seekers like me? Crew from the William*? Spanish sailors seeking to reclaim their cargo?* The bones were piled in front of a smaller, mouse-hole shaft that led into complete darkness. Beside the pile of bones was a larger, nicer, partially used torch. Lighting another of Turtle Bill's striking sticks, I touched the torch and kicked the spent one he'd made aside.

Trying not to think about what would happen if I got stuck, I crawled forward.

Except getting stuck in the small, narrow shaft was all I could think about. Rough stone raked across my shoulders. The back of my head kept bumping against fang-like protrusions. It goes without saying that the shaft was too tapered to turn around, so I won't mention it.

Deep breaths, Ricky, deep breaths.

Scrambling forward as fast as I could, I emerged into a cavernous room. Another partially spent torch was wedged into the wall next to my head. *So I'm not the first visitor.* I touched mine to the charred nub, and the room glowed with light.

Storage trunks of all sizes lay stacked against one wall. So many I couldn't count. Several had rusted and rotted through, scattering their contents. Silver dishes, gold coins, red rubies, emerald stones, and white pearls so large they looked like marbles. I'll be honest: I was pretty excited. I mean, it's not every day you sail to a ghost island that cannot be found and come across a cave full of treasure chests.

Lying on top of the mound of treasure was a leather journal. I flipped through a few pages. Most of the entries were in Spanish. Judging from the numerals, though, I decided it was probably the ship's manifest. Which meant the *Nuestra Señora De Riqueza* treasure was real. And meant the drunken parrot was telling the truth. And meant the old fisherman I'd met after I fell into the creek across from our apartment was also telling the truth. I flipped to the last page of the manifest.

There, scrawled across the top of the page, was a warning written in English to:

The poor soul who finds this treasure. What shall it profit a man, if he shall gain the whole world, and lose his own soul?

Not wanting to climb back out in the pitch-black darkness, I hurried back through the shaft, climbed the rickety ladder, and rushed to the cave's entrance.

"Bill, you up there? I found it. I found the treasure. It's here just like you said!"

I waited for his answer. When he didn't reply, I leaned out, but not too far because, you know, I didn't want to fall off and die.

"You up there? It's just like you said. It's here. The treasure."

Still no reply.

"Come on. Stop messing around."

I leaned out a little farther.

"We're going to need some way to get all this stuff out. Those trunks are rotted through."

At last Turtle Bill's face appeared over the rim of The Skull. It was not the face of a man who had just learned that he had found a whole cave full of Spanish treasure.

"S-s-s-sorry, m-m-mate, truly I am."

His stuttering had returned, which as I'm sure you know by now, was not a good sign.

"Had no choice, truly I didn'."

It took me a few seconds to realize what Turtle Bill meant by "no choice." Then I saw it.

Or rather did not see it.

The rope was gone!

CHAPTER TWENTY-FOUR

AT THE END OF MY ROPE

A hand appeared on Turtle Bill's shoulder. Along with the hand was part of the sleeve of a blue coat. Seeing the hand and coat did not leave me with what you would call a *good feeling*.

"I must say, Bradshaw, I felt certain that tale you told at your trial was purely to save your neck. I had no idea you actually believed in such foolishness."

The commodore. I tore my gaze from the blue coat sleeve above. On the empty beach below two longboats crowded with soldiers were making their way around the rocky point that marked the end of our cove. Down the coast a Union Jack fluttered above treetops.

"I could have captured you at any time, Bradshaw. Thought about it, actually, and almost did the night the *Dead Calm* sank from under you. But I wanted my fiancée to believe she might really escape. It's so much better to crush someone's spirit when they're young and naïve. Scars them for life. Kills their soul. And it makes them so much easier to manage in marriage later."

"She doesn't love you."

"Little matter that makes. It is her father's blessing I seek, not her heart. His name and his title as governor."

I said nothing. Not because it was the smart move, which it was, but because all my focus was on trying to find a way to warn Rebecca.

"I should take you back to Port Charles and hang you. That was my intent. But did you know that individuals who spend long stretches of time in solitary places lose their mind? I have witnessed this in some of the inmates in my fort. Why, there is one poor soul who does nothing but face his cell's back wall all day, mumbling. He has been confined six years. Six years, that's how long he has gone without seeing the sun or enjoying the smells of the sea or feeling a breeze on his face. This will be easier and save me the trouble."

Seemed odd that he hadn't mentioned the treasure. Maybe now that he knew its location, he planned to come back for it later and keep it all for himself. Were I the commodore and I captained a British warship, that's what I'd do.

"You will starve, of course," he was saying. "Unless you die of thirst, first. I doubt you will live long enough to go totally mad. Of course, you could jump. Who knows, you may survive the fall. What do you think, Bill? Do you think the lad can survive the fall?"

"Oh, God, please, no!"

Turtle Bill suddenly pitched forward in a headlong, somersaulting plunge. Blue sky framed his outstretched arms; long gray hair streamed upwards. He went sailing past me so close I could see the terror on his face, hear the flapping of his frock. He plummeted end over end and landed with a sickening, muffled *humph*, his body impaled on jagged rock and reef. No gasping moan, no final cry for help. Only the crashing waves breaking onto the rocks interrupted the silence.

"It would appear that jumping from that ledge is not recommended. I would dearly love to continue our chat, but I need to gather your crew and be on my way back to Port Charles."

"There's treasure."

"I know."

"I can help you bring it up."

"Believe me, Bradshaw. The next time I see you, you will be in no condition to help."

For a moment, I thought there might still be time to warn Rebecca. Then one of the older boys emerged from the jungle. He trudged onto the beach with shoulders slumped and wrists bound. Behind him was another. And another. One by one, all the children exited the jungle. Trailing behind them came Rebecca.

Had I been trapped in a fairy-tale story instead of a pirate nightmare, I would have done something brave and bold, not to mention stupid, like suddenly found a rope I had overlooked. Then I would have tied it to a rock, and swung down like Tarzan and saved the day.

But I didn't have a rope, and my absence seizure was not a fairy tale episode that was ending happily. All I could do was watch the soldiers force Rebecca into one of the longboats.

I watched until the warship's white sails disappeared beneath the eastern horizon. I kept looking until the empty blue sea turned black. I knew I would never see Rebecca again. She was gone—this time for good. She had trusted me to look after her and take care of the kids. I had promised I would, gave her my word. But it turned out my word wasn't any better than my father's.

So I guess that's something we have in common, Dad. Thanks a lot.

CHAPTER TWENTY-FIVE

DEAD MEN TELL TALES

Dear Reader: *As you can probably tell by now, this is not going to be a story with a happy ending. I wish it were otherwise. I wish I could tell you that by using my wits and skills, I miraculously scaled down The Skull's rock face, hailed a ship, and sailed back to Port Charles where I prevented Rebecca from marrying Commodore Spotswood. Unfortunately, my travails—an AP English exam word that means "engaged in painful, laborious, and fruitless efforts"— left me stuck in this cave without any means of escape.*

If only I'd gone to heaven the night I drowned. (At least I think I drowned. From the way the paramedics worked on me, I sure looked dead.) But no, I silently asked the Big Guy upstairs to be sent back so I could stay with Mom. Big mistake. Huge. Let me just say: if you ever find yourself dead and offered a chance to go to heaven, GO! Fly there as fast as you can, because I gotta tell you, sticking around after you're dead is hell on earth.

"Hell is a quiet profane word. Are you quite sure your readers will not take offense?"

I sat on the ledge with my feet dangling over the side. Behind me, William Shakespeare rested his back against the wall, legs outstretched, ship's manifest ledger in his lap. The moon's light batched my tubby scribe in a yellowish glow, making him appear almost ghost-like—which, as you will read in a moment—makes perfect sense.

"Are you sure I'm dead?"

"Quite."

"I don't feel dead."

"Souls like ours living on this side of the grave never do. But dead we be. Want that I should draw a little skeleton of you? Would only take a moment."

I thought about his offer for like, oh, two seconds and shook my head. It was hard to tell if he was kidding, but what he said made sense. Like, when we were on the rafts, I was the only one who never really got tired or hungry or thirsty. So either I was in really good shape, which was pretty much impossible, or I was, like William Shakespeare said, dead.

"You're saying I've been dead from the time I fell into the creek until now?"

"Quite." William Shakespeare looked anxiously towards the back of the cave. "Wouldst it be possible to view the treasure, now? That is, after all, why I stowed away on Black Spot's ship and waited in the jungle for him and his men to leave."

"And here I thought when you climbed down that rope you were coming to save me."

"Oh, 'tis true! I am saving thy soul from eternal damnation."

"Well if that's so, how come you tossed the rope away as soon as your big backside landed on the ledge?"

"It is all part of the plan."

"What plan?"

"The one you do not know about, yet."

I almost commented about how dumb that sounded but decided to keep quiet. Arguing with the ghost of William Shakespeare was like … well … stupid. I mean, he's a ghost!

"What would happen if I jumped?"

"I would not recommend thou attempt such a foolish thing."

"If I'm not going to die, why not try it?"

My scribe sighed. "There is so much thou needs to learn about hell. None of it good." He turned a page in the ledger and continued reading.

A few things you should know about hell. For one, hell is real. I'm sure some of you are thinking there's no such thing as hell. Maybe you think there's not a heaven, either. I was a septic. But that's the way it is when you're healthy and young and have your whole life ahead of you. You think you'll live forever and don't worry about what comes next.

"Hang on, did you say 'septic'?"

"Let me see … *There's no such thing as hell. Or heaven. I was a septic.* Yes, that is what you told me to write."

"I'm sure I said skeptic. Septic means infected, diseased, festering."

"S-k-e-p-t-i-c. Got it."

He made the correction with his quill and continued.

But hell is real. It's nothing like what I imagined it would be, though. I've yet to see a fiery lake or anyone gnashing teeth, though it could be I'm in a different part of the neighborhood. From what I can tell, hell is pretty much the same as life except that some part of my body always hurts.

"And this, my young friend, is why thou wouldst be advised to keep away from that ledge. The fall will only bring about more pain, not death."

"But I bet it'd be a rush."

"And lead to more regrets. That is a summation of hell: a place filled with regrets."

"Read on, please."

In hell, I'm constantly regretting some decision I made or thing I said. Not to mention that I'm really, really lonely.

"What about me?" my scribe asked.

"You're a ghost."

"Not a ghost, a spirit. There's a difference."

"You can't be serious?"

"Want that I should explain the intricacies of souls, spirits, and ghosts? Or do you want me to read your story back to you?"

"Story."

In hell, nothing ever works out for the best. You know how sometimes you'll have a bad day, and someone will tell you to look for the silver lining? There's nothing good in hell, no silver lining. In hell, things go from bad to worse to horrible. Like these cuts on my legs and arms. None of them heal, not ever. They just fester and ooze pus and hurt all the time.

"You want me to change 'fester' to 'septic'?"

"Fester is a good word. Leave it. By the way, how come your body isn't all beat-up and bleeding like mine?"

"I avoid perilous and strenuous and harmful activities. Preserving my good looks, I am. Have something of a reputation with the ladies."

"You?"

"Do not cast down thine eyes in that manner. A portly shape is a sign of virility in some parts."

The tide was out and the moon high. Far below lay the misshapen lump that had been Turtle Bill. His body lay where it landed, impaled on rocks. Each time a wave receded, the surge lifted his arm, making it appear as though he was waving up at me.

"Hast thou found thy father yet?"

"*Dost thou* see my father in this cave?"

"No need to be derisive. I merely wondered if perhaps he is down there with the treasure."

Treasure. That's all these pirates care about. Even the dead ones like William Shakespeare. It figured he would have snuck aboard the commodore's ship and sailed to Coffin Cay. And to think for a few moments I actually believed he'd climbed down to save me.

"Sounds as though thou art still harboring bitterness toward him." William Shakespeare put aside the ledger and joined me on the stub-shelf outside the cave's entrance. I hoped his weight wasn't too much. I didn't want to fall. Especially not after I'd learned that any pain I felt would last forever.

He placed his arm around my shoulder the way my basketball coach does (or did before I died) when he was about to give me some gentle advice. "I would have thought after all thou hast been through—losing the dog, ship, girl, orphans, old woman, Turtle Bill—that thou would have forgiven thy father for mistakes. After all, didst thou not promise the governor's daughter thou would come back? And yet thou did not. Now, she is with that scoundrel, Black Spot. What a horrid affair that must be for her. And what of those orphans? I suspect they feel betrayed by you, as well."

If he was trying to make me feel guilty, it wasn't working. "What I did isn't the same, not even close. Dad walked out on us. At least I *tried* to help."

"Whatsoever thou shalt bind on earth shall be bound in heaven: and whatsoever thou shalt loose on earth shall be loosed in heaven."

"Is that some dead philosopher you're quoting?"

"For with what judgment ye judge, ye shall be judged: and with what measure ye mete, it shall be measured to you again."

"Your point?"

"Ye hath the power to save those we love. Or hate. What say you, my young friend? Will you forgive your dad?"

DEAD CALM, BONE DRY

Before I could explain how idiotic crazy he sounded speaking in British gibberish code, William Shakespeare shoved me off the ledge!

For a half-second, I thought it was some kind of dream: like maybe William Shakespeare hadn't just done what I thought he'd done. But the next moment I was flipping in slow motion head over heels towards where Turtle Bill's body lay pinned among the rocks.

Never trust a pirate fixated on finding treasure, I thought. *Not even one passing himself off as William Shakespeare.*

I landed on the sharp, jagged rock-reef with a bone-shattering thud. A pain like nothing I'd ever experienced paralyzed me. I tried to scream, but a wave broke over me, pounding me onto the rocks. I couldn't move, couldn't breathe, but boy, could I feel the tearing of skin and breaking of bone. When the wave's surge receded I blinked away saltwater. William Shakespeare stood on the ledge, looking down, his round body bathed in moonlight. Another surge lifted my body free of the rocks, pulled me away from shore, and plunged me into the depths of the sea.

CHAPTER TWENTY-SIX

The Secret Place

Twilight.
Gentle rain falls onto cobblestones.
Mist cloaks a narrow street hemmed in by a tall rock wall covered in ivy. Beyond two wrought-iron gates, shrouded by vaporous tendrils, lies an ornamental garden with trees and flowering bushes.

I stand before one of the gates without any memory of how I arrived. Why, I'm not sure. I seem to be waiting for something. There is no past, no future, only the present. Dusk seems to go on forever. The mist leaves me neither wet nor chilled. I feel nothing. When I look down, I see why. I have no feet, no legs, *no body*. I exist without shape or form.

"You going in?"

The voice startles me. I whirl, at least I think I pivot, but see no one. Long, slanting stone walls frame the alley behind me.

"I haven't decided, myself," The Voice says. "Thought I might wait to see what kinds of bodies they're issuing today."

Bodies? Who's issuing bodies?

"They are. In there. Didn't you read the sign?"

When the young man speaks, a burst of vapors explode. His words appear like a warm breath on a cold, damp night.

Sign?

"Over the gate?"

I study the small words chiseled into the stone archway above the gate.

> *Your frame was not hidden from Me when*
> *I made you in the Secret Place:*
> *When I wove you together in the depths of the earth.*
> *I saw your unformed body.*
> *All your days were written in*
> *My Book before one of them came to be.*

"I hope I get a lot of days," The Voice says. "I hear some only get a few. You know what kind of body you want? I do. I picked mine out already. Saw a fellow wearing exactly what I wanted right over there by that big rose bush. There are lots of bodies to pick from. If you need help deciding, let me know. I've seen all of them, I think."

I have a body. Or did.

"What happened to it?"

I'm ... not sure.

"Hey, you're not one of those misfits, are you? I've heard of them. Never seen one myself. I hear they sometimes complain that they're in the wrong type of body. Is that why you came back? Because you think your body was a mistake?"

Came back? I've never been here before.

"Sure you have. We all have. You just probably don't remember. How was it? Having a body? Bet it was nice. I've seen others wearing theirs for the first time. They'll show off, strutting around that garden in there like it's the grandest thing to wear a body. Lots of colors and shapes to choose from. What sort of body did you have?"

A beat-up one.

"I meant what color, how large?"

Sort of an off-white, like those flower petals. More thin than round.

"Will you get the same style? If it were me, I wouldn't. I would get something different. I like trying new things. Maybe when you see some of the other styles, you'll decide you want a new style. They practice in that garden, you know."

Who?

"The souls who get new bodies. You'll see them bumping into trees and hedges, stumbling around. Funny looking things, they are. Then, when they get the hang of walking and jumping, they'll up and leave. I don't know where they go. Never had one come back. Except you. How long did it take you to get comfortable wearing your body?"

I don't ... I'm not sure. I always remember wearing being in a body. Until right now, anyway.

"Hey, look. There's a soul with his new body. I wish I could wave him over. Waving is going to be one of the first things I learn to do."

I strain to see through the tendrils of mist swirling about the garden. *I don't see anything except that landscaped hedge, those orange trees, and a kind of mossy ground cover.*

"Right there, by that rose bush. It's coming toward us. Never seen one do that before."

A man comes striding toward me through the mist. He wears a khaki work-shirt with the top two buttons undone, faded jeans stained with oil or dirt, and a red bandana around his neck. Brown boots, a salt-and-pepper flattop haircut, and a tan weathered face with a square jaw.

He stops on the other side of the gate and looks straight at me with the bluest of eyes. "Let it go, Ricky. Let go of the anger."

Dad?

"Your mom misses you. I miss you. Forgive me for not being there for you. I want to come home."

And just like that, everything around me becomes cold, dark, silent. Now there is nothing. A sense of desperate loneliness overwhelms me, and I know, somehow, this is the way I will always be: dark, alone, and desperate for love.

CHAPTER TWENTY-SEVEN

Back from the Dead

"Rick ... he. Rick ... he."
Still dark, still cold, brain foggy. But now a wobbly wheel rattles like maybe someone is pushing a cart through the Secret Garden. Voices murmur.

"If toucan hear me, wheeze Thailand."

Immediately my thoughts go back to the hut with Earl the Butcher; I make a fist. At least I think I make a fist. I can't be sure.

"Good, Ricky, berry good." The hand beneath mine slips away. A thumb lifts one eyelid. Bright light blinds me. I track the light from left to right. Thumb lifts my other eyelid. I follow the light as before. Brightness clicks off.

"How do you feel, Ricky?"

I open both eyes, squinting at the harsh light. An orderly or nurse or doctor stands over me.

Confused. Tired. "Fine," I say.

"Mind if I examine you?" The orderly or nurse or doctor pulls down the sheet, pulls up my gown. "Tell me if anything hurts."

I stare at the ceiling while he pushes my stomach, thumps my chest. Then it hits me. *I have a body! And I'm not in a hut, or a pirate's cave, or the Secret Garden.* The machine beside me beeps. A clip of some kind pinches my finger. While he pokes and prods, I glance at the label on the water pitcher next to my bed. SENTARA REGIONAL MEDICAL CENTER, WILLIAMSBURG, VA.

"Can you sit up for me?"

He presses the drum of his stethoscope against my back. I expect him to ask about the cuts and bruises from where I landed on the rocks at the base of The Skull, but he doesn't.

"Breathe in." I inhale. "Now out."

Can't believe how tired I am. It's like I've been doing wind sprints at basketball practice.

"Again."

Another deep breath.

"Okay, you can lay back." Gown goes down; bed sheet comes up. "Think you're up for company?" I nod. "Great. I'll let the nurses know."

As he opens the door to leave, I ask, "What day is it?"

He hesitates and with a sad sort of sympathetic smile, says, "Christmas. Welcome back, Ricky."

CHAPTER TWENTY-EIGHT

Fake flakes fall on Graceland

"How long was I ... you know, out of it?" I stand next to my bed wearing new jeans and gray cotton socks, a too large tee from a discount clothing store and a thick blue hoodie that's making me sweat.

Mom tucks in a corner of the sheet on my hospital bed and then flattens the wrinkles. I'm sure she knows the hospital will strip the bed and clean the sheets, but Mom obsesses when she's stressed.

"Not long."

"I saw the paramedics working on me. Did I die?"

"Can we talk about something else?" She fluffs the pillow.

"I'd really like to know, Mom. It's sort of a big deal."

"A neighbor saw you fall in the creek, ran over and pulled you out." She flattens out a wrinkle on my hospital bed. "That's all they told me."

Mom doesn't look at me when she says this. I can tell by the hitch in her voice she's hanging on by a thread. We are waiting for someone to bring a wheelchair so they can roll me out. I feel fine. Tired, but fine. I can walk just fine, but Mom says it's a hospital rule that I get rolled out in a chair. Dumb hospital rules.

"How about the doctor? What's he think happened to me?"

Mom sighs. Mom's good at sighing. She can sigh so loud and long that sometimes she sounds like an eighteen-wheeler settling into a parking lot. "By the time I got here, they already had you in this room. Apparently, the paramedics told the ER staff that you were in shock and that's why you weren't responding to their questions. But then the doctor noticed in your medical records that you have epilepsy. Honestly, son, I'm not sure what happened. They haven't told me. I only know you were out for a long time and that's not good."

Mom is about to lose it, so I don't ask her anything else. There'll be time for questions later.

"Oh, hey, I almost forgot." Mom reaches into her purse. "I bought a stocking stuffer for you while I was in Memphis."

"Bet it's a snow globe."

"Ricky, you peeked!"

"No, Mom, I swear." I'm not about to explain how I know what I thought I know, so I say, "When you called, you told me you got me a gift. I figure it has to be a snow globe."

"Here," she says, sounding disappointed.

I take the gift bag from her and hold it up to my head like a fortune-teller. "Bet it has Elvis on the front porch and Priscilla and Ed Sullivan peeping out the window."

"You *did* peek!"

Smiling at her, I look inside the bag. The snow globe looks exactly like the one I'd seen in the hut on the beach. I give it a shake and watch plastic flakes fall onto the green plastic lawn of Graceland. "It's perfect. You're the best mom ever."

That puts her over the edge: eyes mist, lower lip trembles. "I'm going to check and see what's up with that wheelchair."

After the door clicks shut behind her, I give the globe another shake. Fake flakes fall on Graceland. I think of Snake, Clean Willie, Earl the Butcher, and Turtle Bill: the old woman, orphans, and Rebecca. Were they real or simply dream-like memories created by my broken brain? They seemed real. The pain felt real. And the fear I felt when I thought I'd lost my soul to the crew of the *Flying Dutchman*, that was definitely terrifying. But it's all good, now. I'm back home with Mom. That's all that matters.

A soft knock on the door causes me to look up from the globe. A man rolling a wheelchair backs his way into the room. He wears a khaki work-shirt, faded jeans, and brown boots. He's not dressed as an orderly or anyone else on a hospital staff. When he turns and fixes his blue eyes on me, my heart skips.

"Your mother said I could roll you out, son. Hope that's okay."

Dad's salt-and-pepper hair is the same as I remember from the Secret Garden: same tan weathered face with the square jaw.

"I have a lot of explaining to do to you and your mom. And I will. But if I could get a hug …"

I rush to Dad and hug him harder than I've ever hugged anyone in my life. My eyes mist, lower lip trembles, and I lose it.

Ship's Log
Isla de Ataúd

The skiff rocks gently on the placid water as we glide into the cove. Dad sits behind me, rowing. Mom leans over the side, watching for coral heads. I sit on the middle bench seat, helping Dad steer us toward the beach. No waves breaking over the reef. The sea is dead calm: not even a ripple.

Yesterday Mom and Dad and me arrived in Haiti, which, during pirate times, was called Hispaniola. Perhaps you've heard of Hispaniola. Hispaniola gets mentioned a lot in pirate movies. I'm not sure why. Maybe because it's close to Tortuga and Tortuga is definitely an island you're going to want to mention if you're making a pirate movie.

This morning the three of us piled into this small, wooden fishing boat at 5 a.m. and motored west, away from the village of Les Trois. On the nautical chart, the island is called Isla de Ataúd, but when I was here with Turtle Bill, Rebecca, and William Shakespeare they called it Coffin Cay. Now, out past the reef, the skipper of the fishing boat naps with his feet propped on the gunwale. He's pulled a straw hat over his eyes to shade his face from the sun.

The skiff's hull bumps the beach, its bow crunches pebbles. Mom crawls out, grabs the boat's bow, and pulls us onto warm sand. The beach is littered with plastic bottles, Styrofoam containers, and other trash. My science teacher says that small turtles and seagulls get their necks stuck in the six-pack rings and die. Seeing all the trash on such a beautiful beach makes me want to find out who was dumping garbage into the ocean and turn them in.

DEAD CALM, BONE DRY

"Which way?"

I nod towards the jungle in the direction of the old goat path Turtle Bill and I had used.

Mom says, "Should I stay here with the boat?"

"Better come with us," I say. "No telling what sort of creatures on this island, now."

"In that case let's pull the skiff up past the tide line," Dad says.

You may be wondering how my dead dad came back to life. Turns out he was never dead.

Not long after Dad left Mom and moved out there had been a bad truck accident outside of Pittsburg and a Richard Bradshaw was killed. Bradshaw's body was burned so badly they couldn't identify him except from dental records. But I guess whoever was in charge of sending over the dental files made a colossal mistake because the guy who died was Richard L. Bradshaw not Richard J. Bradshaw. Seems weird that two men with similar names would get their teeth cleaned at the same dentist, but that's what happened.

On our drive home from the hospital Dad said, "I nearly choked on my beer when I saw my face splashed across the screen. Almost picked up the phone right then and called your mom. But then I thought about the insurance. Even though we were divorced, your mom was still on the life insurance policy. That's insurance fraud, claiming to be dead when you're not."

Mom was pulling out of the hospital parking lot; I was in the backseat. Dad had turned half way around in the passenger seat so he could talk to me.

"I've hired an attorney to see if he can help me sort this out. I don't want to go to jail. I know I'll have to pay back the money your mom got. But at the time of the accident, me staying dead seemed like the best thing for everyone."

"So why come back now?" Sitting in the backseat I saw Mom's eyes in the rearview mirror and knew from the way she glanced over at Dad that they had talked about how he'd answer that one.

"I wish I could say I knew, son, but honestly, I have no idea. Maybe it had something to do with it being Christmas. I thought about you two all the time. I was such a jerk. Your Mom was right to kick me out. Somehow, knowing I was dead to you two made me want to be a better person. Like I could start over. I stopped drinking. Stopped doing a lot of other things that I'm not proud of. But every time I thought about calling your mom, I got worried about what the insurance company would do to me. Until last night, that is. In my apartment watching *Christmas Vacation* all by myself, I had this feeling that I needed to do the right thing and live with the consequences. Even if that meant going to jail. So I packed a bag and started driving. Wasn't until I got to your mom's apartment this morning that I learned about the fire and what happened to you."

Back on Isla de Ataúd we reach the old goat path. It's hardly a path at all. More like some weeds parted in places where an animal *may have* walked. I've thought a lot about what happened to Dad and why he came back. It's great having him back, like it's an answered prayer. But I can't help but wonder if me seeing him in the Secret Garden is in some way connected to his return.

Mom holds Dad's hand as I lead them up the trail.

Mom has changed and in a good way. Before, when it was just the two of us, she was always on edge. I guess she had to be that way because it was just her and me, and with my epilepsy, she could never relax. Now with Dad around she's more at ease. She even laughs at Dad's jokes, which are really lame.

Dad has our climbing gear in his backpack. For the past few months the three of us have been practicing climbing and belaying on indoor rock walls. Rock-climbing is our new family hobby.

DEAD CALM, BONE DRY

We reach the summit. The wind-blown tree is gone. Some of the boulders are still there, but the curved dome of the skull looks different than I remember it. I scale down and wait for Mom. When she reaches the ledge I grab her ankles and pull her into the cave. Within minutes all three of us are standing next to the pit that was filled with bones. The old wooden ladder is gone. I figure it would be. A lot of rot can happen to a ladder in three hundred years. Dad breaks a glow stick and drops it. No skulls, no skeletons. No scraps of clothes. I try not to hide my disappointment.

"Well?" Dad says. "Is it still worth climbing down?"

"There's a shaft in the pit that leads to a smaller chamber. I should probably check to make sure."

"I'll wait here," Mom says unnecessarily. Like I expect her to climb down into a pit where dead men's bones once were. She's really being a trooper about all this, but Dad and I both know she's anxious to get off this island and back to our hotel.

"Holler if you find anything," Dad says. This is his way of saying, *Hurry and find us some pirate gold!*

I break another glow stick and toss it up the shaft, then begin crawling to the greenish glow. You may be wondering why we went to all the expense of flying to the Dominican Republic, crossed into Haiti and rented a boat for a day to check out a ghost island. To be honest, we needed the money. Since Dad was never actually dead and Mom spent all his life insurance, we have to pay it back. Except like pretty much always, we're broke. So this trip to Isla de Ataúd is our one chance to strike it rich and pay off the debt.

Crawling on bare knees I reach the treasure room. Empty. No surprise there. If the skeleton remains are gone, it figures the treasure would be too. I blame William Shakespeare. He probably took it all. But it could have been the commodore. Or someone else. If the drunk parrot in the settlement upriver of Spanish Town told that tale to everyone who came into the grog shop there's no telling how many sailors tried to find this place. And the old fisherman had warned that every boy in Bristol knew the story of the dog with the longitude and latitude of a ghost island. Any one of them could have found it.

With my phone I snap a few pics of the empty treasure room. My friends back home still don't believe I traveled back in time. Maybe this will convince them, but I doubt it. I return to the pit and climb out.

"Anything else we need to see?" Mom asks me. "Or do?"

Dad wanders back to the entrance and gets a worried look on his face. The wind has picked up, and the fishing boat anchored just beyond the reef is beginning to bounce as whitecaps build. We need to leave pretty soon if we're going to make it back without getting soaked or swamped.

"You believe me, right?"

Dad looks at me with that sad, worried face parents get when they're afraid there's something wrong with their child.

"Of course, son. Look, you found the island and cave, didn't you? How could you have done that if you hadn't been here before? Don't worry about the money. Your mom and I will find some other way to pay back the insurance company, won't we?"

I don't know if Dad is saying that just to make me feel better or if he really believes it. Since he's been back, we've been to church almost every Sunday. Sometimes, before I leave for school, I'll see him reading his Bible. He hasn't said much about what happened to him Christmas Eve night when I fell into the creek. Only that he felt as if God was forgiving him for all the bad stuff he'd done.

"William Shakespeare has taken the treasure," I say. "He wasn't in the best of shape, but I guess even a fat, balding playwright pirate ghost can carry one gold bar at a time if he takes his time. And he had lots of time after he pushed me from the ledge."

"Really, buddy, in the big scheme of things, paying back that insurance money is not a huge deal. It'll all work out, I'm sure of it."

"I did find this," Mom says, coming from the back of the cave.

She holds a moldy, ledger book—one so badly worn and faded that it hardly looks like the ship's manifest that I remember. My heart begins to race.

"Where'd you get that?"

"Back near that hole," Mom says, handing it to me. "Was shoved into a crevice so far I almost didn't see it."

Green mold covers the front and edges of the pages of the small, moldy, leather journal. The pages are yellowed, and the blue ink is faded to light gray, but I can still make out the numerals and Spanish writing showing the exact course and route and dates the *Nuestra Señora De Riqueza* sailed all those hundreds of years ago. After the last entry in the book a new page begins, this one written in English.

> *The leaky, wooden ship bashes into another wave, sending a shudder down the length of its hull. I cling tightly to the bars of my prison cell and study the places where iron shackles have worn my skin raw. Another rush of salty bilge water sloshes up to my calves and recedes, stinging my open wounds. The ship's brig reeks of urine and feces.*

"It's my letter to Mom," I say. "I was dictating my story to William Shakespeare right before he pushed me off that ledge. I guess he added it from memory." Quickly I skim the rest of the pages. "It's all here, the whole story. Even the parts I never told William Shakespeare. How's that possible?"

"You know what this means?" I say to my parents. "Means I really was right here in this cave."

"But we already knew that," Dad says.

"I think what your father is trying to say, honey, is that everything you experienced really happened."

"And if it can happen once," Dad says to me, "it could happen again. You could end up right back here in the land of pirates and buried treasure."

"But let's hope it *doesn't*," Mom says. "I never want to go through that again."

But of course it will. Of that I'm sure.

THE END

www.ingramcontent.com/pod-product-compliance
Lightning Source LLC
Chambersburg PA
CBHW021438080526
44588CB00009B/583